CLEOPATRA

CLEOPATRA

Dorothy and Thomas Hoobler

CHELSEA HOUSE PUBLISHERS
NEW YORK
PHILADELPHIA

CUER
DT
92.7
.H66
1986

SENIOR EDITOR: William P. Hansen
PROJECT EDITOR: John W. Selfridge
ASSOCIATE EDITOR: Marian W. Taylor
EDITORIAL COORDINATOR: Karyn Gullen Browne
EDITORIAL STAFF: Maria Behan
        Susan Friedman
        Pierre Hauser
        Perry Scott King
        Kathleen McDermott
        Howard Ratner
        Alma Rodriguez-Sokol
        Bert Yaeger
LAYOUT: Irene Friedman
ART ASSISTANTS: Noreen Lamb
        Carol McDougall
        Victoria Tomaselli
COVER ILLUSTRATION: Teresa Clark
PICTURE RESEARCH: Susan Quist

Frontispiece courtesy of Art Resource/Alinari

Revised Edition
   5 7 9 8 6 4

Library of Congress Cataloging in Publication Data

Hoobler, Thomas. CLEOPATRA.

(World leaders past & present)
Bibliography: p.
Includes index.
  1. Cleopatra, Queen of Egypt, d. 30 B.C.—Juvenile
literature. 2. Egypt—Queens—Biography—Juvenile
literature. [1. Cleopatra, Queen of Egypt, d. 30 B.C.
2. Kings, queens, rulers, etc.] I. Hoobler,
Dorothy. II. Title. III. Series.
DT92.7.H66   1985   932′.02′0924 [B] [92] 85-6611

ISBN 0-87754-589-8
    0-7910-0624-7 (pbk.)

Contents

JOHN ADAMS
JOHN QUINCY ADAMS
KONRAD ADENAUER
ALEXANDER THE GREAT
SALVADOR ALLENDE
MARC ANTONY
CORAZON AQUINO
YASIR ARAFAT
KING ARTHUR
HAFEZ AL-ASSAD
KEMAL ATATÜRK
ATTILA
CLEMENT ATTLEE
AUGUSTUS CAESAR
MENACHEM BEGIN
DAVID BEN-GURION
OTTO VON BISMARCK
LÉON BLUM
SIMON BOLÍVAR
CESARE BORGIA
WILLY BRANDT
LEONID BREZHNEV
JULIUS CAESAR
JOHN CALVIN
JIMMY CARTER
FIDEL CASTRO
CATHERINE THE GREAT
CHARLEMAGNE
CHIANG KAI-SHEK
WINSTON CHURCHILL
GEORGES CLEMENCEAU
CLEOPATRA
CONSTANTINE THE GREAT
HERNÁN CORTÉS
OLIVER CROMWELL
GEORGES-JACQUES
  DANTON
JEFFERSON DAVIS
MOSHE DAYAN
CHARLES DE GAULLE
EAMON DE VALERA
EUGENE DEBS
DENG XIAOPING
BENJAMIN DISRAELI
ALEXANDER DUBČEK
FRANÇOIS & JEAN-CLAUDE
  DUVALIER
DWIGHT EISENHOWER
ELEANOR OF AQUITAINE
ELIZABETH I
FAISAL
FERDINAND & ISABELLA
FRANCISCO FRANCO
BENJAMIN FRANKLIN

FREDERICK THE GREAT
INDIRA GANDHI
MOHANDAS GANDHI
GIUSEPPE GARIBALDI
AMIN & BASHIR GEMAYEL
GENGHIS KHAN
WILLIAM GLADSTONE
MIKHAIL GORBACHEV
ULYSSES S. GRANT
ERNESTO "CHE" GUEVARA
TENZIN GYATSO
ALEXANDER HAMILTON
DAG HAMMARSKJÖLD
HENRY VIII
HENRY OF NAVARRE
PAUL VON HINDENBURG
HIROHITO
ADOLF HITLER
HO CHI MINH
KING HUSSEIN
IVAN THE TERRIBLE
ANDREW JACKSON
JAMES I
WOJCIECH JARUZELSKI
THOMAS JEFFERSON
JOAN OF ARC
POPE JOHN XXIII
POPE JOHN PAUL II
LYNDON JOHNSON
BENITO JUÁREZ
JOHN KENNEDY
ROBERT KENNEDY
JOMO KENYATTA
AYATOLLAH KHOMEINI
NIKITA KHRUSHCHEV
KIM IL SUNG
MARTIN LUTHER KING, JR.
HENRY KISSINGER
KUBLAI KHAN
LAFAYETTE
ROBERT E. LEE
VLADIMIR LENIN
ABRAHAM LINCOLN
DAVID LLOYD GEORGE
LOUIS XIV
MARTIN LUTHER
JUDAS MACCABEUS
JAMES MADISON
NELSON & WINNIE
  MANDELA
MAO ZEDONG
FERDINAND MARCOS
GEORGE MARSHALL

MARY, QUEEN OF SCOTS
TOMÁŠ MASARYK
GOLDA MEIR
KLEMENS VON METTERNICH
JAMES MONROE
HOSNI MUBARAK
ROBERT MUGABE
BENITO MUSSOLINI
NAPOLÉON BONAPARTE
GAMAL ABDEL NASSER
JAWAHARLAL NEHRU
NERO
NICHOLAS II
RICHARD NIXON
KWAME NKRUMAH
DANIEL ORTEGA
MOHAMMED REZA PAHLAVI
THOMAS PAINE
CHARLES STEWART
  PARNELL
PERICLES
JUAN PERÓN
PETER THE GREAT
POL POT
MUAMMAR EL-QADDAFI
RONALD REAGAN
CARDINAL RICHELIEU
MAXIMILIEN ROBESPIERRE
ELEANOR ROOSEVELT
FRANKLIN ROOSEVELT
THEODORE ROOSEVELT
ANWAR SADAT
HAILE SELASSIE
PRINCE SIHANOUK
JAN SMUTS
JOSEPH STALIN
SUKARNO
SUN YAT-SEN
TAMERLANE
MOTHER TERESA
MARGARET THATCHER
JOSIP BROZ TITO
TOUSSAINT L'OUVERTURE
LEON TROTSKY
PIERRE TRUDEAU
HARRY TRUMAN
QUEEN VICTORIA
LECH WALESA
GEORGE WASHINGTON
CHAIM WEIZMANN
WOODROW WILSON
XERXES
EMILIANO ZAPATA
ZHOU ENLAI

ON LEADERSHIP

Arthur M. Schlesinger, jr.

LEADERSHIP, it may be said, is really what makes the world go round. Love no doubt smooths the passage; but love is a private transaction between consenting adults. Leadership is a public transaction with history. The idea of leadership affirms the capacity of individuals to move, inspire, and mobilize masses of people so that they act together in pursuit of an end. Sometimes leadership serves good purposes, sometimes bad; but whether the end is benign or evil, great leaders are those men and women who leave their personal stamp on history.

Now, the very concept of leadership implies the proposition that individuals can make a difference. This proposition has never been universally accepted. From classical times to the present day, eminent thinkers have regarded individuals as no more than the agents and pawns of larger forces, whether the gods and goddesses of the ancient world or, in the modern era, race, class, nation, the dialectic, the will of the people, the spirit of the times, history itself. Against such forces, the individual dwindles into insignificance.

So contends the thesis of historical determinism. Tolstoy's great novel *War and Peace* offers a famous statement of the case. Why, Tolstoy asked, did millions of men in the Napoleonic Wars, denying their human feelings and their common sense, move back and forth across Europe slaughtering their fellows? "The war," Tolstoy answered, "was bound to happen simply because it was bound to happen." All prior history predetermined it. As for leaders, they, Tolstoy said, "are but the labels that serve to give a name to an end and, like labels, they have the least possible connection with the event." The greater the leader, "the more conspicuous the inevitability and the predestination of every act he commits." The leader, said Tolstoy, is "the slave of history."

Determinism takes many forms. Marxism is the determinism of class. Nazism the determinism of race. But the idea of men and women as the slaves of history runs athwart the deepest human instincts. Rigid determinism abolishes the idea of human freedom—

the assumption of free choice that underlies every move we make, every word we speak, every thought we think. It abolishes the idea of human responsibility, since it is manifestly unfair to reward or punish people for actions that are by definition beyond their control. No one can live consistently by any deterministic creed. The Marxist states prove this themselves by their extreme susceptibility to the cult of leadership.

More than that, history refutes the idea that individuals make no difference. In December 1931 a British politician crossing Park Avenue in New York City between 76th and 77th Streets around 10:30 P.M. looked in the wrong direction and was knocked down by an automobile—a moment, he later recalled, of a man aghast, a world aglare: "I do not understand why I was not broken like an eggshell or squashed like a gooseberry." Fourteen months later an American politician, sitting in an open car in Miami, Florida, was fired on by an assassin; the man beside him was hit. Those who believe that individuals make no difference to history might well ponder whether the next two decades would have been the same had Mario Constasino's car killed Winston Churchill in 1931 and Giuseppe Zangara's bullet killed Franklin Roosevelt in 1933. Suppose, in addition, that Adolf Hitler had been killed in the street fighting during the Munich *Putsch* of 1923 and that Lenin had died of typhus during World War I. What would the 20th century be like now?

For better or for worse, individuals do make a difference. "The notion that a people can run itself and its affairs anonymously," wrote the philosopher William James, "is now well known to be the silliest of absurdities. Mankind does nothing save through initiatives on the part of inventors, great or small, and imitation by the rest of us—these are the sole factors in human progress. Individuals of genius show the way, and set the patterns, which common people then adopt and follow."

Leadership, James suggests, means leadership in thought as well as in action. In the long run, leaders in thought may well make the greater difference to the world. But, as Woodrow Wilson once said, "Those only are leaders of men, in the general eye, who lead in action. . . . It is at their hands that new thought gets its translation into the crude language of deeds." Leaders in thought often invent in solitude and obscurity, leaving to later generations the tasks of imitation. Leaders in action—the leaders portrayed in this series—have to be effective in their own time.

And they cannot be effective by themselves. They must act in response to the rhythms of their age. Their genius must be adapted, in a phrase of William James's, "to the receptivities of the moment." Leaders are useless without followers. "There goes the mob," said the French politician hearing a clamor in the streets. "I am their leader. I must follow them." Great leaders turn the inchoate emotions of the mob to purposes of their own. They seize on the opportunities of their time, the hopes, fears, frustrations, crises, potentialities. They succeed when events have prepared the way for them, when the community is awaiting to be aroused, when they can provide the clarifying and organizing ideas. Leadership ignites the circuit between the individual and the mass and thereby alters history.

It may alter history for better or for worse. Leaders have been responsible for the most extravagant follies and most monstrous crimes that have beset suffering humanity. They have also been vital in such gains as humanity has made in individual freedom, religious and racial tolerance, social justice, and respect for human rights.

There is no sure way to tell in advance who is going to lead for good and who for evil. But a glance at the gallery of men and women in *World Leaders—Past and Present* suggests some useful tests.

One test is this: Do leaders lead by force or by persuasion? By command or by consent? Through most of history leadership was exercised by the divine right of authority. The duty of followers was to defer and to obey. "Theirs not to reason why / Theirs but to do and die." On occasion, as with the so-called enlightened despots of the 18th century in Europe, absolutist leadership was animated by humane purposes. More often, absolutism nourished the passion for domination, land, gold, and conquest and resulted in tyranny.

The great revolution of modern times has been the revolution of equality. The idea that all people should be equal in their legal condition has undermined the old structure of authority, hierarchy, and deference. The revolution of equality has had two contrary effects on the nature of leadership. For equality, as Alexis de Tocqueville pointed out in his great study *Democracy in America,* might mean equality in servitude as well as equality in freedom.

"I know of only two methods of establishing equality in the political world," Tocqueville wrote. "Rights must be given to every citizen, or none at all to anyone . . . save one, who is the master of all." There was no middle ground "between the sovereignty of all and the absolute power of one man." In his astonishing prediction of 20th-century totalitarian dictatorship, Tocqueville explained how the revolution of equality could lead to the *"Führerprinzip"* and more terrible absolutism than the world had ever known.

But when rights are given to every citizen and the sovereignty of all is established, the problem of leadership takes a new form, becomes more exacting than ever before. It is easy to issue commands and enforce them by the rope and the stake, the concentration camp and the *gulag.* It is much harder to use argument and achievement to overcome opposition and win consent. The Founding Fathers of the United States understood the difficulty. They believed that history had given them the opportunity to decide, as Alexander Hamilton wrote in the first Federalist Paper, whether men are indeed capable of basing government on "reflection and choice, or whether they are forever destined to depend . . . on accident and force."

Government by reflection and choice called for a new style of leadership and a new quality of followership. It required leaders to be responsive to popular concerns, and it required followers to be active and informed participants in the process. Democracy does not eliminate emotion from politics; sometimes it fosters demagoguery; but it is confident that, as the greatest of democratic leaders put it, you cannot fool all of the people all of the time. It measures leadership by results and retires those who overreach or falter or fail.

It is true that in the long run despots are measured by results too. But they can postpone the day of judgment, sometimes indefinitely, and in the meantime they can do infinite harm. It is also true that democracy is no guarantee of virtue and intelligence in government, for the voice of the people is not necessarily the voice of God. But democracy, by assuring the right of opposition, offers built-in resistance to the evils inherent in absolutism. As the theologian Reinhold Niebuhr summed it up, "Man's capacity for justice makes democracy possible, but man's inclination to injustice makes democracy necessary."

A second test for leadership is the end for which power is sought. When leaders have as their goal the supremacy of a master race or the promotion of totalitarian revolution or the acquisition and exploitation of colonies or the protection of greed and privilege or the preservation of personal power, it is likely that their leadership will do little to advance the cause of humanity. When their goal is the abolition of slavery, the liberation of women, the enlargement of opportunity for the poor and powerless, the extension of equal rights to racial minorities, the defense of the freedoms of expression and opposition, it is likely that their leadership will increase the sum of human liberty and welfare.

Leaders have done great harm to the world. They have also conferred great benefits. You will find both sorts in this series. Even "good" leaders must be regarded with a certain wariness. Leaders are not demigods; they put on their trousers one leg after another just like ordinary mortals. No leader is infallible, and every leader needs to be reminded of this at regular intervals. Irreverence irritates leaders but is their salvation. Unquestioning submission corrupts leaders and demeans followers. Making a cult of a leader is always a mistake. Fortunately hero worship generates its own antidote. "Every hero," said Emerson, "becomes a bore at last."

The signal benefit the great leaders confer is to embolden the rest of us to live according to our own best selves, to be active, insistent, and resolute in affirming our own sense of things. For great leaders attest to the reality of human freedom against the supposed inevitabilities of history. And they attest to the wisdom and power that may lie within the most unlikely of us, which is why Abraham Lincoln remains the supreme example of great leadership. A great leader, said Emerson, exhibits new possibilities to all humanity. "We feed on genius. . . . Great men exist that there may be greater men."

Great leaders, in short, justify themselves by emancipating and empowering their followers. So humanity struggles to master its destiny, remembering with Alexis de Tocqueville: "It is true that around every man a fatal circle is traced beyond which he cannot pass; but within the wide verge of that circle he is powerful and free; as it is with man, so with communities."

1

The Early Years

In the nurseries of the later Ptolemies one learned early the realities of life, the hardships of power, and the devious windings of statecraft.
—ERNLE BRADFORD
modern historian

In the year 41 B.C., a man and a woman met in the city of Tarsus, in Asia Minor (part of modern-day Turkey). The man was Marc Antony; the woman was Cleopatra. Their meeting was to have far-reaching consequences — for the history of the Roman Empire and hence for the history of the Western world. But the story of their romance has often overshadowed even the historical importance of their meeting. It is a story of passionate love and the lust for power.

At the time Antony met Egypt's Queen Cleopatra, he was one of the three members of the Roman triumvirate that ruled the Mediterranean world. He had sent several letters and emissaries to Cleopatra, summoning her to his presence, but she had chosen to keep him waiting. This was a daring step, for she possessed no real military power, while Antony had the legions of Rome at his disposal.

Shrewdly she calculated her arrival so as to flaunt the riches of her kingdom as well as her striking personal mystique. Up the river Cydnus toward Tarsus she sailed in a boat with a stern of gold, its purple sails billowing in the wind while slaves slapped silver oars against the water in time to the

THE BETTMANN ARCHIVE

Writing more than a century after Cleopatra's death, Plutarch, the Greek historian, described her as the siren of the Nile, a scheming woman who caused Antony's tragic downfall. This somewhat biased view influenced all subsequent biographies, for earlier Egyptian records of her life were destroyed by the Romans.

Cleopatra VII (69–30 B.C.), the last queen of Egypt, used all her wiles and charms in her attempt to restore the greatness that Egypt had possessed under earlier rulers. The two child rulers shown in this mosaic from an ancient tomb governed Egypt 1,300 years before Cleopatra gained her throne.

music of flutes, pipes, and lutes. Cleopatra reclined on the deck, costumed as Aphrodite, the Greek goddess of love and beauty. Boys costumed as Cupid, the god of love in Roman mythology, fanned her with colored ostrich plumes. The crew of the boat, at the rudder and sails, were Cleopatra's beautiful handmaidens, also dressed as mythological figures. As the boat drew near the city, rich perfume emanated from burning censers and wafted its fragrance to the banks of the river. Multitudes lined the banks to see this wonder, rushing along to follow the boat's progress. It was a masterpiece of theater, and the crowd was enchanted.

Antony, at first unaware of Cleopatra's approach, sat in the marketplace of the city, receiving those who wanted favors from him. Gradually, as word spread, people drifted away until Antony was left alone with his soldiers. He was too proud to join the admiring throngs at the river. But he sent a message to Cleopatra, asking her to join him for dinner. Cleopatra, determined to maintain the upper hand, turned down his invitation, but also suggested that he join her for dinner on her boat instead.

When Antony arrived, he was immediately impressed. The floating palace, decorated with illuminated lanterns hanging from branches, looked like an enchanted forest. Inside there were embroidered dining couches and tables set with golden plates and goblets. It is said that after a magnificent feast Cleopatra presented all of the golden dishes and fine embroideries to Antony as a little gift.

The next evening, Antony tried to prepare as lavish a banquet as Cleopatra had. He did not succeed. He had a good sense of humor, though, and quickly turned his failure as a host into a joke. When Cleopatra realized that Antony was less sophisticated than she was, she smoothly altered her behavior to match his.

Cleopatra had succeeded in charming Antony. It was not great beauty that made men like Antony fall in love with Cleopatra. Although she was very attractive, it was her intelligence, wit, and charm that captivated Antony. Plutarch, a historian who lived about a hundred years after Cleopatra, tried

The barge she sat in, like a burnish'd throne,
Burn'd on the water: the poop was beaten gold;
Purple the sails, and so perfumed that
The winds were love-sick with them.

—WILLIAM SHAKESPEARE
poet and dramatist,
describing Cleopatra's
barge in his play *Antony
and Cleopatra*

to explain her allure: "The charm of her presence was irresistible, and there was an attraction in her person and her talk, together with a peculiar force of character which pervaded her every word and action, and laid all who associated with her under its spell."

Cleopatra, whose name in Greek meant "glory of her race," was born in 69 B.C. in Alexandria, the capital of Egypt. Her father, Ptolemy XII, was the ruler of Egypt. He had a number of titles as part of

When Cleopatra set sail to meet Marc Antony in Tarsus, he represented the world's greatest military power, but she represented one of the world's oldest civilizations. This model of a pleasure craft used by Egyptian royalty dates from the 14th century B.C.

his name — Theos Philopator Philadelphus Neos Dionysos — meaning "the God, Lover of the Father, Lover of his Sister or Brother, the New Dionysus." Among his subjects, Ptolemy XII was known by the more familiar name, Auletes, meaning "the flute player."

The musicians of Cleopatra's golden boat struck a rich historical note, for by 3500 B.C., while western Europe was still in the Stone Age, Egypt had produced the flute, followed by the harp, double clarinet, and lyre, pictured here in a wall painting from a tomb.

Ptolemy Auletes had two wives, and it is uncertain which of them was Cleopatra's mother. It was probably Cleopatra Tryphaena, who was both the wife and sister of Auletes. Since the beginning of their dynasty, the Ptolemies had frequently ruled as brother and sister, husband and wife.

Cleopatra had two younger brothers, born in 61 and 59 B.C., and she would eventually marry each of them in turn, continuing this tradition of family rule. She also had two older sisters — another Cleopatra Tryphaena and Berenice — and a younger sister, Arsinoë. All would play a part in the struggle for power that marked Cleopatra's younger years.

It was Alexander of Macedon, known as Alexander the Great, who was responsible for the succession of the Ptolemy dynasty to the throne of Egypt. Alexander had conquered most of the known world in his brief lifetime — from his homeland north of Greece, east to India, and south into Africa. He had

Alexander the Great, on horseback, in one of the several battle scenes portrayed on his stone coffin. At the time of his death, his empire extended from Greece to India and included Persia, which would later become Parthia, and Egypt. Cleopatra dreamt of restoring such imperial greatness to Egypt.

founded the city of Alexandria on the Mediterranean Sea, and it was here that he was buried.

After Alexander's death in 323 B.C., his empire was divided between three Macedonian families. The Ptolemies took Egypt, the Antigonids controlled Macedonia and much of Asia Minor, and the Seleucids ruled an empire that included Syria and the lands farther east. These three kingdoms made up the Hellenistic world. The language of trade was Greek, as was the predominate culture.

At their capital of Alexandria, the Ptolemies were active patrons of that culture. Ptolemy I had established a library and museum where scholars from all over the Mediterranean world came to study. By Cleopatra's time, the library contained over 700,000 volumes.

Much of what remains of the great literature, philosophy, and science of Greece came to the modern world through Alexandria. It was in Alexandria that Eratosthenes became the first man to measure the circumference of the earth, and the scientist Aristarchus formulated the theory that the earth revolves around the sun. It was here that Euclid systematized geometry and wrote his *Elements of Geometry*. His ideas form the basis of what is taught today in high school. (The first Ptolemy asked Euclid if geometry could be made easier to learn. Euclid's famous answer was "There is no royal road.")

Alexandria, the capital of Egypt, the burial place of Alexander the Great, was one of the most extraordinary creations of that far from ordinary man.
—ERNLE BRADFORD
modern historian

Cleopatra spent most of her life in Alexandria. A remarkable and fascinating place, it was the scene of many of her greatest triumphs, and of her ultimate defeat. Alexander the Great had picked this site for his capital because of its magnificent harbor. In the middle of the harbor was Pharos Island, at the tip of which was one of the Wonders of the Ancient World — a lighthouse whose fire, magnified by mirrors, could be seen 35 miles out to sea. A mole, or causeway, connected the island and the mainland, dividing the harbor into two sections. To the east was the Great Harbor; to the west, the Safe Return Harbor. A series of canals connected the harbor to the Nile River.

On the shore facing the Great Harbor was the palace, a complex of buildings where Cleopatra was

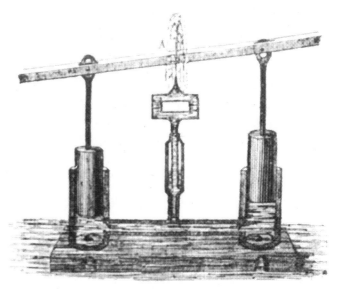

born and spent her childhood. Here were magnificent gardens, the royal tombs, the museum and library, and temples to both Egyptian and Greek gods. Cleopatra grew up accustomed to the finest of luxuries, imported from all over the known world.

Alexandria's main street, Canopic Street, crossed the city from east to west. Traders from many countries brought their goods to the shops and bazaars that lined the street. Many different languages, from the Mediterranean area and from countries as far away as India, could be heard there. Cleopatra, a brilliant linguist, was able to speak many of these languages fluently.

Alexandria was famous for its manufacture of luxury goods, such as perfumes, papyrus, fine ivory, jewelry, and glass vases. Its streets were filled with entertainers such as mimes, musicians, tricksters, and roving philosophers. At the Hippodrome, which could hold 20,000 spectators, there were chariot races and plays.

The city abounded with temples devoted to both Egyptian and Greek gods. Some elements of the Greek religion had fused with Egyptian beliefs. The presiding deity of the city was the Graeco-Egyptian

god Serapis, for whom the Serapeum temple was built. Serapis was said to communicate with people in dreams, which were then interpreted by oracles at the Serapeum. Since the oracles were employed by the Ptolemies, Serapis's "messages" were likely to be favorable to the ruling regime.

In an attempt to consolidate their power over the country, the early Ptolemies adopted some of the practices of the pharaohs, or rulers of ancient Egypt. One such practice was the deification of leaders. Cleopatra claimed to be Isis, the Egyptian goddess of motherhood and fertility. With her brother Osiris, Isis was ruler of the earth and sky. The Ptolemies' custom of brother-sister marriage was also derived from the practices of the ancient pharaohs.

Because the pharaoh was divine, he was literally the owner of Egypt. The Ptolemies appointed Greek overseers to run the country's agriculture. Egypt's wealth stemmed from its rich farmland along the Nile. The choice of crops, care of animals, innovations in farming methods, and major projects such as irrigation, canal construction, and road building all fell under the personal control of the ruler. The palace complex at Alexandria included the govern-

The first libraries appeared in Egypt around 2500 B.C. The library in Alexandria, one of the greatest the world has ever known, burned to the ground during Cleopatra's lifetime. Ironically, an illustration of an Egyptian fire engine pump (left) escaped the flames, and from it the model shown here was constructed.

ment offices from which the country was administered. Papyrus, unique to Egypt, made it possible to keep convenient and portable records (unlike the unwieldy baked clay tablets used in other cultures), and this helped the system run efficiently.

But the Ptolemies traditionally had little to do with the people of Egypt, except to demand their labor and agricultural production. The Egyptians lived as they had for centuries, keeping their own religion with its myriad gods, goddesses, and sacred animals.

The first three Ptolemies were vigorous rulers. In addition to Egypt, they conquered Cyrenaica (part of modern Libya), much of Palestine, the eastern Mediterranean coast, and the island of Cyprus, as well as portions of Asia Minor. But then the dynasty declined and they lost most of their overseas possessions. One of Cleopatra's goals was to regain much of the empire of the early Ptolemies.

For some time before Cleopatra's birth, the rising power of Rome had been threatening the system established by Alexander's successors. Roman forces had conquered the Antigonids and taken part of the kingdom of the Seleucids. Along with the island of Cyprus, Egypt itself still remained under the control of the Ptolemies. Thus, the major task of Ptolemy Auletes, Cleopatra's father, and later Cleopatra herself, was to maintain Egypt's independence from Rome through skillful diplomacy.

Cleopatra's father had ascended to the throne in 80 B.C. when the resentful people of Alexandria murdered his predecessor, who had been despised primarily because he gained the throne with the help of the Roman dictator Sulla. More and more, without actually invading Egypt, the rulers of Rome had come to play a greater part in its affairs.

Cleopatra's father found himself in an awkward position. His kingdom was split when his brother became king of Cyprus. His troubles increased when it became known that his predecessor, Ptolemy XI, had left a will ceding Egypt to Rome.

It might seem strange that Rome did not take advantage of Ptolemy XI's will by immediately sending troops into Egypt. Rome, however, was having

We who today are filled with admiration of the Roman conquests which introduced Latin culture into countries inhabited by barbarians ought not to forget that the people thus favored regarded the matter very differently. All they saw of Latin culture were the legionaries who threatened their existence, the tax-farmers who extorted money from them, and the officials who enriched themselves without scruple.
—OSKAR VON WERTHEIMER
modern historian

GIRAUDON/ART RESOURCE

An Egyptian pharaoh was entombed in this gold coffin
in the 14th century B.C. Declaring themselves god-kings,
Egypt's pharaohs reigned more than 2,500 years, until
the land was conquered by the Persians in 525 B.C. When
the Ptolemies assumed the rulership of Egypt, they declared themselves god-kings too and adopted the ways of
the pharaohs.

its own troubles.

For several hundred years Rome had been a republic governed by an elected senate, which appointed two consuls to administer the government each year. In cases of emergency, such as war, the consuls could appoint a dictator who became the absolute ruler of the state for a limited period. In reality, the real rulers of Rome were those who controlled the army, which governed the conquered territories that brought the empire so many of its vast riches.

One of the problems of Rome's republican government was corruption. Men appointed to govern Rome's rich provinces often used the opportunity to enrich themselves. In the past, military officers

> *In Rome men had forgotten what honesty was. A person who refused a bribe was regarded not as an upright man, but as a personal foe.*
> —THEODOR MOMMSEN
> modern historian

had built up their armies abroad, later returning to Rome to seize power. The Roman Senate came to the uncomfortable realization that there was no one it could truly trust with the riches of Egypt. Therefore, it served the Senate's purposes to allow Cleopatra's father to remain on the throne of Egypt.

In the year 60 B.C., when Cleopatra was nine years old, three men combined their forces to establish a triumvirate to restore order to Rome and its empire. These men were Marcus Crassus, Gnaeus Pompey, and Julius Caesar. Pompey and Caesar were military heroes, while Crassus was among the wealthiest men in Rome.

Pompey had made his name as a military commander by defeating the Seleucids and annexing

Egypt's wealth flowed from the Nile and the fertile land in the river valley. Increasing nature's bounty, the Egyptians developed new farming techniques, including the use of plows, rakes, manure, and irrigation systems. In this harvest scene, royal servants measure and record crop results for their palace report.

Syria as a Roman province in 64 B.C. This had brought him uncomfortably close to Egypt, and Auletes, Cleopatra's father, sent him presents of money and military supplies in order to stay in his good graces.

After the triumvirate was formed, Auletes went to Rome in 59 B.C. and urged Pompey to use his influence to allow Egypt to remain independent. The other two triumvirs, Crassus and Caesar, were in favor of annexing Egypt. Auletes showered influential senators with presents of gold and eventually managed to strike a deal with Caesar, who needed money to reward his soldiers and begin preparations for a new military campaign. To buy off Caesar, Auletes borrowed a large sum of money from a Roman financier, Rabirius Postumus. In exchange for the money, Caesar persuaded the Senate to pass what became known as the Julian Law. It called Ptolemy XII Auletes an "ally and friend of the Roman people." Egypt's independence, along with Auletes's hold on the throne, was saved — at least for a time.

Auletes's brother, the ruler of Cyprus, did not fare as well. The Romans decided the time was right to seize his island kingdom, traditionally a part of the Ptolemaic domain. Auletes made no protest, and when the Roman forces took control of Cyprus, Auletes's brother committed suicide. His treasure was promptly added to the Roman coffers.

The people of Alexandria were unhappy that their king had done so little to aid his brother. They were even more unhappy when it became known that Auletes expected them to pay back the money he had borrowed from Rabirius Postumus. The Alexandrians rose up in revolt, and Auletes fled, leaving his elder daughters Cleopatra VI Tryphaena and Berenice as co-regents in his absence. Cleopatra VI died not long after, and Berenice assumed control herself.

Auletes turned to his Roman friends for help. He first went to Cato, the new Roman governor of Cyprus. In a calculated insult, Cato remained seated while receiving the Egyptian king. He gave the deposed king some unpleasant advice: Auletes's plans to appeal to the Roman Senate were doomed be-

Later to become Rome's greatest military hero, Julius Caesar began his career as a lawyer. As a member of the first triumvirate, the ruling coalition he established with Marcus Crassus and Gnaeus Pompey in 60 B.C., Caesar favored the invasion of Egypt, but Cleopatra's father, Auletes, bought him off with borrowed money.

cause, "All Egypt turned into gold would no longer satisfy the greed of the Roman politicians." He suggested that Auletes return to Alexandria and concentrate on pacifying his people.

Auletes knew this was impossible without a supporting force of Roman legionaries, so he continued on to Rome. Pompey declined to help him, and Caesar was far to the north, on the campaign that would result in the defeat of Gaul (modern-day France).

Berenice decided to send her own representatives to Rome, to ensure that her father would not get the help he sought. Auletes outwitted his daughter by hiring assassins who murdered her envoys when they arrived in Italy.

Postumus, the Roman financier who had lent Auletes the money, was becoming increasingly con-

The Romans acquired their wealth through military conquest. As the empire expanded, Rome's elected government was increasingly dominated by the men who led and financed the armies. Pictured here in an engraving, the Roman Forum, or open market square, was the focal point of government, public spectacles, and political intrigue.

In 59 B.C., fearing for his life, Auletes abandoned his throne, and Cleopatra's older sister, Berenice, assumed control. This royal throne was used by an Egyptian queen of an earlier period.

cerned that he would not get his money back unless Auletes regained control of Egypt. With Postumus's help, Auletes once again liberally spread presents and bribes throughout Rome. The Senate seemed to grow favorably disposed toward Auletes.

The Senate consulted the Sybilline Books on the matter. These were prophetic books kept at the temple of the Roman goddess Sybil. The oracle of the books proclaimed, "If the king of Egypt comes asking for help, do not refuse him friendship, but do not go to his aid with a host or you will meet with troubles and dangers." The Sybil may have accurately reflected the true feeling of the Roman Senate.

Auletes was not yet finished, however. Leaving an agent in Rome, he went to Ephesus (in Asia Minor) and contacted the Roman governor of Syria, Aulus Gabinius. He offered Gabinius a staggering sum in gold to restore him to the throne of Egypt.

The Sybil had forbidden direct help to the king of Egypt, but the gold was persuasive enough to help Gabinius discover a different reason for military action. He charged that Berenice's husband was encouraging pirates off the North African coast.

Soon a Roman army was streaming south from Syria toward the Egyptian border town of Pelusium. The cavalry was led by a young officer named Marc Antony. The Roman legions broke rapidly through all resistance, occupied Alexandria, and restored Auletes to his throne. He immediately had his daughter Berenice put to death. This took place in 55 B.C., when Cleopatra was 14. Fortunately for her, she was as yet too young to take a role in politics, but she was learning that cunning and ruthlessness could be effective political tools.

Some of Gabinius's soldiers remained in the city to keep order. Marc Antony stayed for a short time, and it is said that the young princess made an immediate impression upon him. He saw for the first time the exciting city of Alexandria, and the palace where one day he would live.

Auletes now began the struggle to pay off the enormous debts he had incurred. Rabirius Postumus, so clearly allied with Auletes's efforts, ventured to Egypt to help him. Postumus was made finance minister of Egypt so that the vast wealth of Egyptian trade passed directly through his hands.

This tranquil state of affairs lasted for only a short time, however, for once more the Alexandrian mob rioted. After an attempt was made to kill him, Rabirius set sail for Rome.

In Rome another discussion took place over whether Egypt should be annexed. In a last attempt to forestall this action, Auletes made a will stating that Cleopatra, ruling with his eldest son, should succeed him, and sent a copy of it to Rome. He begged the Senate to see that his will was enforced, and named the Roman people as the guardians of the new king and queen.

In 52 B.C. the Alexandrians consecrated their city to Auletes and his children. The following year Auletes died. Cleopatra, known as Cleopatra VII, ascended the throne with her younger brother,

Auletes's brother, the king of Cyprus, committed suicide when Roman troops invaded the Mediterranean island and raided the royal treasury. The people of Alexandria rose up in arms when they learned the king of Egypt had done very little to defend him. This gold headpiece is from a late Ptolemaic coffin.

Auletes resumed his reign with the help of Roman legions
led by Marc Antony. A Roman mosaic composed of colored tiles portrays the arrival of Roman officers at a temple on the Nile.

Ptolemy XIII. She was 18 years old and her brother only 10. They were formally married, in Egyptian custom, but there is no evidence that they ever really lived as husband and wife.

In her 18 years, Cleopatra had witnessed her father's desperate struggle to keep his throne. We do not know where she lived during her sister's brief reign, but she must have been aware that it was Rome's soldiers who put her father back on the throne. Now she would have to make use of what she had learned.

From this point on, Cleopatra would show herself to be tireless and clever. After growing up in a corrupt court where the struggle for power was pervasive, she was also ruthless. Well aware of the former greatness of the Ptolemies, she yearned to restore their empire.

In many ways Cleopatra resembled the early Ptolemies. Throughout her reign she patronized the arts and sciences, and often attended the scholarly discussions in the palace museum. She was the first Ptolemaic ruler to learn the language of her subjects, the Egyptians.

One of her first acts as ruler was designed to make her popular with the Egyptian people. She was aware that they held their gods and goddesses in high esteem, and she attempted to associate herself with the Egyptian deities whenever possible. The priests of the Egyptian religion, with their shaven heads and linen robes, occasionally appeared at court, and the Ptolemies sometimes made contributions to their temples.

Cleopatra hit on a striking gesture to show her sympathy for the Egyptians' deepest beliefs. One of the holy places in southern Egypt, Hermonthis, kept a live bull named Euchis as its local god. In the first year of Cleopatra's reign, the bull died, and a new one was installed with high ceremony. Cleopatra apparently traveled upriver to participate in the ceremony personally. An inscription at the shrine says, "The Queen, the Lady of the Two Lands, the goddess who loves her father, rowed the Bull in the Barge of Amon to Hermonthis."

However, Cleopatra soon faced a threat within the

It seems that from the very first she displayed the strength of character and political intelligence which were to be so evident throughout her life.
—ERNLE BRADFORD
modern historian

Hoping to increase her popularity with her subjects, Cleopatra provided a shrine in southern Egypt with a new bull of Hermonthis when the old bull died. *The Seven Celestial Cows and the Sacred Bull* appear in this mural.

royal palace. Because her brother was a minor, he ruled with the assistance of a regency council. His three most important advisers were his Greek tutor, Theodotus; the minister of finance, Pothinus; and the commander of the army, Achillas. They perceived, quite rightly, that Cleopatra was a threat to their rule of Egypt. They could control the young Ptolemy XIII, but Cleopatra was stronger willed and would not surrender her power to them without a fight.

A combination of factors which bred unrest, among them a bad harvest that led to a famine, gave the regency council enough power to oust Cleopatra from the throne. She eventually made her way to the eastern Mediterranean. There, like her father before her, she found backers who were willing to provide support in return for a chance to share in the riches of Egypt. Cleopatra raised an army in Syria and marched down the coast to Pelusium. Here, her forces faced those of the advisers acting in her brother's name. But the battle never took place. Once again, events in Rome determined who finally gained control of Egypt.

In a wall painting from a pharaoh's tomb, wailing women cry for bread. In 48 B.C., when Egypt's harvest failed, the resulting famine created political unrest, which was aggravated by Ptolemy XIII's advisers. The young Queen Cleopatra was driven into exile by her brother's supporters.

2

Caesar and Cleopatra

Cleopatra was taking a desperate gamble. Even though she had done well to raise an army to support her cause and showed personal courage by accompanying the troops to battle, later events prove that her insistence on taking part in the military planning irritated the male commanders. Cleopatra lived in a world in which military matters, in fact, all matters of government, were left to men. Therefore, she not only had to overcome her country's political weakness, but prejudice against her as a woman as well. Her brother Ptolemy XIII's ruling council may have let her go because they thought she was harmless; but now that they perceived her as a threat, her defeat would mean certain death.

Cleopatra's accomplishments in a man's world were due in part to her ability to attract, and to use, men. But she had no way of knowing that the most powerful man in the Mediterranean world would shortly come into her life. To understand how that came about, we must return to Rome.

The triumvirate established in 60 B.C. had by this time dissolved. Crassus had sought military glory with an invasion of the Parthian Empire (roughly the combined area of Iran and Iraq), but was de-

GIRAUDON/ART RESOURCE

The golden eagle, a bird of prey, adorned the battle standards with which the Roman legions marched to victory east and south throughout the Mediterranean and north as far as Britain. In Gaul (France), Caesar won lasting fame as a brilliant military strategist.

As Julius Caesar's mistress, Cleopatra acquired a reputation as an exotic and irresistible temptress, but she appears quite prim and proper in this rare, true-to-life Graeco-Roman sculpture.

feated at Carrhae in 53 B.C., losing his life along with 30,000 of his men.

Carrhae was one of the worst military defeats in Roman history. The disgrace of the Parthian king's capture of the golden eagle standards, or banners, of the Roman legions burned in the minds of Romans. Both Julius Caesar and Marc Antony were eventually to plan an invasion of Parthia to erase this stain on Roman honor.

The death of Crassus brought Caesar and Pompey into conflict. Pompey seemed to have the better position, for he controlled Rome, while Caesar was still in Gaul with his army.

In 49 B.C. Caesar brought his forces across the Rubicon River, the dividing line between the Gallic provinces and Italy. Knowing this action meant war, Caesar remarked, "The die is cast." Since Pompey had no desire to meet Caesar in battle until he had increased the strength of his own forces, he retreated across the Adriatic Sea.

Among the places Pompey looked to for help was Egypt. In 49 B.C., while Cleopatra was still ruler,

Gnaeus Pompey, known as Pompey the Great, began his military career while still in his teens and had risen to the rank of general by the age of 25. Later Caesar and Pompey served together in Rome's first triumvirate.

THE BETTMANN ARCHIVE

Pompey's son Gnaeus appealed for grain and military help. Cleopatra sent 60 ships loaded with grain and 500 men from the Gabinian forces still in Alexandria.

Caesar continued his pursuit of Pompey, telling his ship's pilot on the voyage across the Adriatic: "Fear nothing; you carry Caesar and his fortune." The fateful battle was fought at Pharsalus in 48 B.C. It was a rout, with Caesar sweeping through all opposition. Pompey did manage to escape, however, and fled to Cyprus. From there he set sail for Egypt, hoping to find refuge.

This occurred just as Cleopatra was preparing to confront her brother's forces at Pelusium. By September 28 Pompey's ship appeared off the coast. He sent a message asking for safe conduct to the ruling council in Ptolemy's camp.

Pompey's arrival forced an uncomfortable decision on the ruling council. If they accepted him, they ran the risk of incurring Caesar's enmity. If they turned him away, however, he was certain to turn to Cleopatra for help. With his forces added to hers, she might well prevail in the forthcoming battle. It was the continual dilemma of Egypt's rulers at this time: they had to be sure of backing the right side in Rome's internal struggles.

Ptolemy's three advisers advanced different strategies. Achillas was for sending Pompey a message to depart. Pothinus wanted to give him an honorable reception. But Theodotus argued for a third approach. "If you receive him," Theodotus said, "you will have Caesar for your enemy and Pompey for your master. If you send him off, Pompey may one day revenge the affront and Caesar will resent your not having delivered him into Caesar's hands. The best solution is to send for Pompey and put him to death." Theodotus cold-bloodedly summed up his argument by pointing out that "dead men do not bite."

Achillas and a former officer of Pompey's took a small boat to Pompey's ship and welcomed him to Egypt. As he stepped into their boat, it is said that Pompey turned to his wife and quoted Sophocles: "Do you seek a tyrant's door? Then farewell free-

Caesar had never hated Pompey. They were both men of great charm, and their purely personal relations had often been warm. Ultimately, however, it had simply been impossible for both of them to occupy the same political position at Rome that each craved.
—FRITZ M. HEICHELHEIM
modern historian

dom!" As soon as Pompey was ashore, he was slain. His wife's screams echoed from ship to shore as she helplessly witnessed his beheading.

A few days later Caesar landed at Alexandria and was presented with Pompey's head and signet ring. Supposedly, Caesar wept at the sight. He was glad to have Pompey out of the way, but was sorry that his death had come at the hands of the Egyptians, whom he considered inferior to Romans.

Caesar now entered the city with a small force of soldiers. The standard-bearers carried aloft the *fasces*, an ax with a bundle of rods which symbolized Roman authority. The people of Alexandria, interpreting the procession as an affront to the Egyptian king, rioted and a large number of Caesar's troops were killed.

Caesar established himself in the palace area of the city, which was easily defended. He claimed that the money Auletes had promised had not been paid in full. He demanded payment, and seemed prepared to wait there until he got it.

Pothinus, the finance minister and chief of the ruling council, treated Caesar with rudeness. When Caesar ordered food for his troops, Pothinus sent moldy grain. Caesar was served his meals on wooden or pottery dishes rather than the gold or silver plates that usually adorned the royal table.

With Pothinus's encouragement, the riots in the city continued. He pointedly suggested that Caesar must have more pressing business elsewhere, alluding to the fact that he still had to consolidate his power in Rome. The possibility exists that the ruling council may even have discussed dealing with Caesar as they had with Pompey.

But Caesar was not a man to be easily frightened. He cited the provisions of Auletes's will that placed his children's welfare in the hands of the Roman Senate. As Rome's representative, Caesar then announced that he would settle the dispute between Cleopatra and her brother. He ordered them brought before him.

The ruling council saw no harm in agreeing, since Ptolemy was not needed with the troops and there seemed to be no safe way for the embattled Cleopatra

Caesar was 42 years old and suffered from epilepsy when
he led his first military campaign, the conquest of Gaul.
His success brought him increasing popularity and
wealth, creating fear in the Roman Senate. When, in 49
B.C., the senate demanded that Caesar disband his troops,
he refused, and invaded Italy.

To strengthen their political bonds, Pompey had married Caesar's daughter, Julia. When she died, the men began the rivalry that led to civil war, and Pompey fled to Alexandria, where the Column of Pompey stands today.

to reach the palace. Ptolemy returned from Pelusium, leaving his soldiers behind to murder Cleopatra if she tried to reach Alexandria.

However, Cleopatra devised an ingenious plan to get to Caesar. With one of her confidants, a Sicilian named Apollodorus, the former queen came down the coast in a small boat and landed near the palace in the early evening. She then had Apollodorus wrap her in "the coverlet of a bed" and carry her through the palace gates to Caesar's apartment.

When Cleopatra was unwrapped, she rose up as if in a fairy tale. Caesar was delighted. It appears that the two became lovers that same night.

The fiery romance between Cleopatra and Caesar has been almost as celebrated in myth and literature as her affair with Marc Antony. (There are numerous paintings, ballets, plays, and movies about Cleopatra and the mystery of her allure. Virgil, Shakespeare, George Bernard Shaw and other brilliant writers have immortalized her.) At the time they met, Caesar was 52; Cleopatra just 19. Caesar was experienced in war, in politics, and by all accounts in love as well. The historian Suetonius describes him as "tall . . . fair-complexioned, rather full-faced, with dark piercing eyes." He was an expert rider since boyhood. Plutarch says, "he had trained himself to put his hands behind his back and then, keeping them tightly clasped, to put his horse to its full gallop. . . . He got himself into the habit of dictating letters on horseback, keeping two secretaries busy at once." Caesar did have a problem with his health, however. According to Suetonius, he had experienced the "falling sickness," what physicians today call epilepsy.

Caesar was a vain man, "nice . . . in the care of his person." Not only did he cut his hair short and keep his face smoothly shaved, but he had the hair on his body plucked regularly as well. Recently he had been growing bald, and his uneasiness about his thinning hair made it a subject of jokes among his foes. Suetonius says that "of all the honors conferred on him by Senate and People there was none he accepted or used with more pleasure than the right of constantly wearing a laurel crown" to hide his baldness.

Cleopatra may have learned much about the world from Caesar, but as we have seen she had shown herself to be shrewd and resourceful long before she met him. The Roman historian Dio Cassius calls her "a woman of surpassing beauty, and at that time, when she was in the prime of her youth, she was most striking."

Caesar's infatuation with Cleopatra soon became apparent to all. The first to discover it was her brother Ptolemy, who was summoned to Caesar's room in the morning. On seeing his sister with Caesar, he ran from the room saying that his cause had been betrayed. He apparently went to his friends, burst into tears, and tore his crown off his head. News that the exiled Cleopatra was in the palace with Caesar spread rapidly. Crowds gathered and began to demonstrate outside the palace, and Caesar's troops seized Ptolemy in the confusion.

> *He often feasted with her until dawn; and they would have sailed together in her state barge nearly to Ethiopia had his soldiers consented to follow him.*
> —SUETONIUS
> Roman historian,
> describing Caesar's
> relationship with Cleopatra

Caesar now made a public reading of Auletes's will and proposed a settlement that must have seemed generous. He called for the resumption of joint rule between Cleopatra and Ptolemy in Egypt. He also gave their younger sister and brother control over Cyprus, which had been a Roman province for the past ten years.

Ptolemy's advisers, disheartened by Cleopatra's restoration, summoned their troops from Pelusium and surrounded Alexandria. Ptolemy, at Caesar's request, called for their dispersal, but his command was ignored.

The poet Lucan described the feast that was held to celebrate Cleopatra's reconciliation with her brother. She was arrayed in fine silks and pearls from the Red Sea. "Great was the bustle as Cleopatra displayed a magnificence not yet adopted in Roman ways." The hall in which the feast was held was "too costly even for an age corrupted with pleasure-spending." The ceiling had rafters covered with gold, the walls were solid marble, and the guests trod on polished alabaster floors.

During this feast, Caesar's barber overheard a conversation between Ptolemy's advisers Achillas and Pothinus in which the two hatched a plot against Caesar's life. Caesar promptly had Pothinus killed. Achillas, however, managed to escape.

Achillas's forces moved to capture Caesar's ships in the harbor, but Caesar had them burned to keep them from falling into his enemy's hands. Meanwhile, Caesar's forces took the island of Pharos so that they could be resupplied from the sea.

Caesar kept accounts of his own campaigns for posterity. Writing in the third person, he described what happened next: "He secured the most necessary points and fortified them in the night. In this quarter of the town was a wing of the palace, where Caesar was lodged on his first arrival. A theater next to the house served as a citadel and commanded an avenue to the port. He strengthened these fortifications in the next few days so that he might have a rampart in front and not be forced into a fight against his will."

Cleopatra's younger sister Arsinoë, unsatisfied

> *I will make all the men I love kings. I will make you a king. I will have many young kings, with round, strong arms; and when I am tired of them I will whip them to death; but you shall always be my king; my nice, kind, wise, good old king.*
> —from George Bernard Shaw's play *Caesar and Cleopatra*, Cleopatra addressing Caesar

The Triumph of Caesar, by the 16th-century Italian painter Andrea Mantegna, depicts Caesar's entrance into Rome, with trumpets blaring and banners flying, parading the riches of conquest. When Caesar entered Alexandria in this fashion, the local population took offense and began to riot.

43

A Ptolemaic ruler from the 1st century B.C. wearing the serpent headdress of the Egyptian pharaohs. According to legend, when Cleopatra's brother saw her in Caesar's bedroom, he tore off his crown and ran from the room in tears.

with Caesar's offer of the Cyprian throne, left the palace and went over to Achillas. However, she and her adviser, Ganymede, quarreled with Achillas. Arsinoë showed her Ptolemaic mettle by having Achillas killed. Ganymede now took command of the troops surrounding Caesar.

Caesar had sent for reinforcements by sea. When these arrived, they attacked the Egyptian fleet. Caesar took his men and rushed onto the mole that led from the mainland to Pharos Island. But the Egyptians surprised him by landing behind him.

The only escape for Caesar's men was to swim for the Roman ships. Caesar, 52 years old, showed his

Avoiding the assassins sent by the ruling council of Alexandria, Cleopatra had herself rolled in a rug, carried through the city, and delivered to Caesar. She made a spectacular first impression when she was unwrapped, the moment envisioned in this 19th-century painting.

physical vigor by swimming to safety, losing only his purple general's cloak.

Caesar now made a calculated move. He released Ptolemy XIII, allowing him to rejoin the Egyptian forces led by Ganymede and Arsinoë. When new reinforcements arrived, Caesar completely defeated the Egyptians. Ptolemy drowned trying to escape.

The next day Caesar marched his troops through Alexandria again. This time the citizens recognized the inevitable. They honored him with the sacred symbols customarily used to mollify their offended kings.

Cleopatra shared in the glory. She was recrowned queen of Egypt, sharing the throne with her young-

est brother, now called Ptolemy XIV. He was only 11 at the time and would thus prove no obstacle to her authority in Egypt. Her sister Arsinoë was banished to Rome.

Caesar, with his fellow triumvirs dead, was now in control of the Mediterranean world. As his lover and protégée, Cleopatra seemed destined for great things indeed.

After the victory, she wined and dined Caesar in appropriately royal fashion. She began construction of the Caesarium, an enormous building on the shore, in his honor. (Cleopatra's Needles, two stone obelisks constructed in 1500 B.C., were moved from their original location to the temple by Caesar's

Horrified by Caesar's decision that Cleopatra should resume her reign as queen, the ruling council of Alexandria decided the time had come to kill him and ordered their troops to surround the city. This battalion of Egyptian wooden soldiers was found in a tomb dating from the 19th century B.C.

47

PHAROS

CVRSIBVS EXTRVXTI RATIVM PTOLEMÆE REGVNDIS   CLARA,
NOCTVRNIS PHARON, VT QVVM NOX TENEBROSA SILERET,   INFIDA.

The lighthouse on Pharos Island in Alexandria's harbor was long considered one of the Seven Wonders of the Ancient World. It was here that Caesar prepared his defense against the ruling council's troops.

IN PHÆBES, VOMERENT FVNALIA LVCEM,
ILI SIC TVTIVS ORA SVBIRENT.

adopted son Octavian some years later. They were brought to England and the United States in the 19th century, and now one stands along the Thames River in London and the other in Central Park in New York City.)

One of the special enjoyments Cleopatra planned for Caesar was a cruise up the Nile in a gigantic pleasure barge. Caesar was a very curious man. He undoubtedly would have wanted to see the farmlands along the Nile and the legendary monuments, temples, and ruins. He also probably wanted to assess Egypt's wealth in order to calculate how much it would add to the value of the Roman Empire.

The royal barge was a floating palace. It was even more lavish than the one on which Cleopatra would later entertain Marc Antony. According to some, it was 300 feet long and 46 feet wide, rising about 60 feet above the water. It contained banquet rooms, courtyards, garden areas, and shrines. The Roman historian Suetonius wrote that at this time Caesar's "greatest favorite was Cleopatra, with whom he often revelled all night till the dawn of day, and would have gone with her through Egypt in dalliance as far as Ethiopia, in her luxury yacht, had

Built in the 27th century B.C., the Pyramids of Giza rise beside the Nile. When this photograph was taken in the 19th century, the Egyptians continued to live much as they did when Caesar viewed the sights from Cleopatra's royal barge.

The coronation scene from a 1906 production of *Caesar and Cleopatra*, by the celebrated British playwright George Bernard Shaw. In this play, Shaw takes a humorous look at the 30-year age difference between the aging Roman leader and his ambitious young mistress.

not the army refused to allow him."

As his military staff probably reminded him, Caesar had problems elsewhere. In Pontus, on the southern shore of the Black Sea, in Asia Minor, King Pharnakes had invaded some surrounding territories which were under Roman control. Caesar quickly marched his forces to the city of Zela. His account of the battle became famous: *"Veni, vidi, vici."* (I came, I saw, I conquered.)

51

Cleopatra, left in Egypt with three Roman legions to protect her, ruled unopposed. According to Plutarch, she bore Caesar a son, Caesarion. Some other historians put the birth at two or three years later; still others argue that she never had a child by Caesar.

We do know that Cleopatra insisted that her firstborn was indeed Caesar's son. In fact, she even had coins struck to commemorate the event. They show her as the goddess Isis holding a baby, Horus-Caesarion. (Horus was the son of the Egyptian gods Isis and Osiris.)

In the year 46 B.C., Cleopatra and Ptolemy XIV went to Rome. This was the year of Caesar's great Triumph, the traditional celebration for victorious Roman generals.

Caesar's Egyptian victory was only one of several that were celebrated at this time. During the period of his absence from Rome, he had also conquered the Gauls, King Pharnakes, and parts of North Africa. The fact that he was now the sole leader of Rome made this Triumph particularly significant.

There were four days of spectacular celebrations. On one occasion Caesar hosted an elaborate banquet for 22,000 people. A wooden amphitheater was erected in the Forum, the public square of Rome. Here Caesar displayed captives and animals that he had brought back from far-off lands. (One of these was a giraffe from Africa, which the people of Rome called a camelopard.) Prisoners of war and gladiators were pitted against each other, as well as against animals — even elephants.

It is not certain if Cleopatra arrived in time for the Triumph. In any case, Egypt was not without a representative, albeit an unwilling one. On the second day, Cleopatra's sister Arsinoë was chained and paraded through the streets of Rome along with paintings of the Nile and Alexandria's Pharos lighthouse. It is probable, too, that Caesar's soldiers sang bawdy but good-natured songs about his dalliance with Queen Cleopatra. They were fond of singing verses such as: "Put away your wives, you men of Rome. We bring the baldhead lecher home."

A short time later Caesar honored Cleopatra in a

more formal ceremony that made clear to all that she was much more than a casual lover to him. He dedicated a new temple to Venus Genetrix, the Roman counterpart of the Greek goddess Aphrodite. Within the temple, Caesar placed a statue of Cleopatra. It is said that when the sculptor was creating this statue Caesar became impatient and asked "How long will it take to finish the job?" The sculptor explained how difficult the project was and estimated that it would take 10 years. Caesar replied, "Make it 10 days!" And so it was. As a further honor, Cleopatra was made a member of Caesar's family.

Rome was scandalized. The Romans' inflated pride caused them to look down on other peoples, even the Greeks from whom their own culture was largely derived. A great deal of the political strife within Rome stemmed from disputes as to how far Roman citizenship should be extended beyond the boundaries of the city itself. Roman citizenship was an honor not lightly given, and it was unheard of to identify a foreigner with a Roman goddess. Caesar added to the controversy by establishing Cleopatra and her brother-husband in his country home outside the city. This seemed an affront to Caesar's wife, Calpurnia, who was famous for her virtue.

As Dio relates, Caesar "incurred the greatest censure of all through his passion for Cleopatra: not what he had shown in Egypt . . . but what was evident in Rome itself. . . . However, he was not at all concerned, but actually enrolled her among the Friends and Allies of the Roman people."

Now that Caesar was supreme, Rome was filled with speculation about his plans. One rumor had it that he was planning to establish a central government in Alexandria. Caesar was perceived as ambitious, energetic, and still in the prime of his physical strength. No one suspected that he had only a year to live.

He first set about reforming many of the outdated aspects of Roman administration and customs. One reform, which stemmed from his stay in Alexandria, was to have a lasting effect on civilization. Caesar seems to have met the astronomer Sosigenes in

To celebrate the birth of her first child, Caesarion, Cleopatra issued a coin depicting herself as Isis, the Egyptian goddess of fertility, who ruled the earth and sky. Cleopatra's son appeared on the coin as the sun god, Horus — the tiny figure here perched on Isis's hand in this late Ptolemaic statue.

The Romans borrowed much of their culture and religion from the Greeks. Aphrodite, the Greek goddess of beauty and love, was known in Rome as Venus. The goddess is depicted here stroking the tail of a dolphin while the god of love, known as Eros or Cupid, holds her towel.

VENERE E AMORE
-GIARDINO CESARINI-

Cleopatra's palace. Sosigenes showed him the calculations that Greek scholars had made regarding the movement of the earth around the sun. Caesar used this knowledge to correct the Roman calendar in the year 45 B.C.

The Romans formerly used a 355-day calendar, with extra months inserted every two years. Because of this, the schedule of crop planting became con-

The Romans began construction on the Appian Way, the world's first paved road, in the 3rd century B.C. This section leads to Rome, where Cleopatra was entertained as Caesar's personal house-guest in 46 B.C., while her sister, Arsinoë, was paraded through the city as a captive.

The Ruins of the Temple of Venus Genetrix in Rome. Many historians believe Caesar contributed to his own downfall when he defied tradition by dedicating the new temple of Venus to Cleopatra and commissioned a statue of her to represent the goddess.

As a young man, Caesar was appalled by the reactionary tyrants who ruled Rome, and he struggled to restore the legal rights of citizens. In his later years, yielding to the temptations of power, he allowed his image to appear on Roman coins inscribed "Caesar God" and "Dictator for Life."

fused. The new calendar had 365 days, with an extra day every four years. (After Caesar's death, the month of his birth, Quintilis, was renamed Julius — today's July.) This calendar (called the Julian calendar) was used throughout Western civilization until the 16th century, when further refinements were made.

Like the calendar, most of the reforms Caesar made were beneficial for Roman civilization. He still made many enemies, especially among the more conservative members of the Roman aristocracy. Caesar was generous with his Roman enemies — for instance, he pardoned most of those who supported Pompey — and this leniency contributed to his downfall.

One rumor spread by Caesar's enemies was that he planned to become king of Rome. In the nations around the Mediterranean, rule by kings was customary. Rome, however, was proud of its republic, and prized simple democratic virtues. In reality, Rome was the capital of a great empire that had been governed for nearly a century by whichever man or group controlled Rome — usually military heroes. Even so, proper form required even dictators to proclaim their support for the republic, and rumors that Caesar scorned the republic damaged his reputation considerably.

The beginning of the year 44 B.C. found Caesar planning a military campaign against the Parthians, to avenge Crassus's defeat at Carrhae. At home, he was beginning a great building program.

On February 15 the annual festival of Lupercal took place. This popular holiday was the remnant of an ancient fertility rite. Young men, chosen to be *Luperci*, would run through the streets naked, playfully striking people with shaggy thongs called *februa*. Any woman touched would supposedly become pregnant that year.

During this particular festival one of the *Luperci* was Marc Antony. After running through the streets, he rushed up to Caesar and offered him a crown. A few of Caesar's supporters applauded. Caesar pushed the crown away and the whole crowd applauded and cheered with delight. They saw this refusal as a sign of Caesar's devotion to the republic.

Some people were not convinced, however. There was a conspiracy forming against Caesar, led by Brutus and Cassius, two ardent republicans. Plutarch says that on the night of March 14 all the doors and windows of the house where Caesar slept with his wife flew open. Calpurnia awoke from a terrible nightmare in which Caesar had been killed. The next day she begged Caesar not to go to the Senate. She felt that her dream was a very bad omen. But Caesar went anyway. On the Ides of March (March 15) the great Caesar was stabbed to death upon entering the Senate. It is said that a great comet shone brightly for seven nights after Caesar's murder and then disappeared, and the sun was dim for a full year.

Cleopatra must have been devastated by the news of her lover's assassination. Not only was her love lost, but all of her dreams for the future. In addition, her own life was now in danger, for the people of Rome had never really accepted her. In the confusion that swept the city, Cleopatra quickly boarded a ship and set off for Alexandria.

> *Caesar hoped that with stability and security assured by his sweeping reforms he would be free to pursue a scheme of conquest that would make him even greater than Alexander the Great.*
> —FRITZ M. HEICHELHEIM
> modern historian,
> describing Caesar's plans
> shortly before his assassination

Fearing that Caesar would abandon the constitutional law of the Roman Republic and establish a monarchy, 60 senators took part in his assassination, depicted here in an 18th-century engraving. In 44 B.C., on the Ides of March (March 15), Caesar was stabbed to death on the steps of the Senate.

3
Antony and Cleopatra

Caesar's assassins thought that his death would bring back the traditional Roman republic in which the Senate was the main body of authority. However, they had no clear plan for achieving their goal, and in the days after Caesar's death Rome was swept with uncertainty and fear.

Soon after Cleopatra's return to Alexandria with her son Caesarion and her husband-brother Ptolemy XIV, Ptolemy was killed, probably by poison, on Cleopatra's orders. Although he posed no threat to her, she was not about to take the chance that he would become one, as his older brother had.

There is no record of disturbances in Alexandria at this time, so we can assume that Cleopatra's rule was successful and popular enough to allow her to overcome the effects of Caesar's death and the murder of her brother. The Roman legions that Caesar had left in Egypt remained, and they were loyal to Cleopatra — at least until events in Rome became stabilized.

But Cleopatra was now in the same precarious situation in which her father had been before her. She was the ruler of a country without a strong military force. Furthermore, her country's rich ag-

Cleopatra's Needle is a monumental *obelisk*, a four-sided stone shaft that tapers to a point and marks the passing hours as its shadow circles around. Placed near a pharaoh's tomb in 1500 B.C., it was later moved to Alexandria and set near the Caesarium, Cleopatra's temple. This obelisk stands in New York City, while its twin is found in London.

Marc Antony mourned Caesar's death with mixed emotions; though he truly grieved, he also expected to succeed him. As Caesar's friend and most trusted officer, Antony was, therefore, stunned when he found himself obliged to share power with Caesar's official heir and adopted son, Octavian.

I have long been sated with power and glory; but, should anything happen to me, Rome will enjoy no peace.
—JULIUS CAESAR
as recorded by the Roman historian Suetonius

Delivering the eulogy at Caesar's funeral, Marc Antony displayed Caesar's torn and bloody robe and aroused public outrage against the assassins. The scene is reenacted in this photograph from a 19th-century production of Shakespeare's tragedy *Julius Caesar.*

riculture made it a prize for whomever was strong enough to march in and take it. All of Cleopatra's skills were required to retain her throne. Before she could take any action, however, she had to await developments in Rome.

Marc Antony, Caesar's greatest friend and lieutenant, had been detained in conversation by one of the conspirators at the door of the Senate when Caesar was killed. On the night after the murder Antony went to Caesar's house and took possession of his will, war chest, and papers.

Aemilius Lepidus, Caesar's Master of the Horse (second-in-command), brought in Caesar's troops to occupy the city and restore order. Caesar's will was read in public, revealing that he had made no mention of Cleopatra or her son.

On March 20 Antony rose to give the oration at Caesar's funeral. We do not know exactly what he said, but 16 centuries later Shakespeare put these famous words in his mouth: "Friends, Romans, countrymen, lend me your ears; I come to bury Caesar, not to praise him." In fact, Antony did praise Caesar, stirring the throngs gathered at the public marketplace. He ended the eulogy by dramatically brandishing Caesar's bloodstained robe. This excited the people to a fury against those involved in the conspiracy. Fearing for their lives, the two main conspirators, Brutus and Cassius, fled the city.

Antony was now the most powerful man in Rome. He held the office of consul, and began to appoint his allies to important offices. The Senate, intimidated by Caesar's troops (which were now loyal to Antony) and the hasty retreat of Caesar's opponents, meekly complied with Antony's actions.

What kind of man was Antony, who was to play such an important role in the life of Cleopatra? Plutarch describes him as follows: "He had a very good and noble appearance. His beard was well grown, his forehead large, and his nose aquiline, giving him a bold, masculine look that reminded people of the faces of Hercules in paintings and sculptures." Antony's physical appearance helped make believable his own claim that he was a descendant of the god Hercules.

[Antony was] a colossal child, capable of conquering the world, but incapable of resisting a pleasure.
—JOSEPH-ERNEST RENAN
French philosopher
and historian

ALINARI/ART RESOURCE

In his will, Caesar named his grandnephew, Octavian, as his adopted son and heir. In death, Caesar was no longer feared but revered, and Octavian promptly took the name Gaius Julius Caesar. Following his example, Roman emperors later assumed the name of Caesar as an honor.

Antony was a hearty man who enjoyed a joke. His soldiers admired him because he shared their meals and joined in their rough conversation — qualities that Roman aristocrats like the orator Cicero despised. Antony was known for his drinking and his easy way with women. He was married to an ambitious woman named Fulvia, who ignored his indiscretions because she enjoyed being the wife of such a powerful and rich man.

Antony was exceedingly generous with all who were close to him. A typical example of his liberality was when he gave orders for a large sum of money that the Romans called a *decies* to be presented to a friend. His steward was so shocked by the size of the gift that he collected the money and laid it out in a heap in front of Antony in order to show him just how much money it was. When Antony saw that the steward begrudged the expense, he remarked, "I thought a decies was more than that. This is just a trifle: you had better double it!"

Caesar's will pronounced his 18-year-old grand-nephew, Octavian, as his heir and adopted son. Octavian hurried to Rome from Greece, where he had been a student. Although at first Antony refused to take Octavian's claims seriously, the young man proved to be a more formidable opponent than Antony had anticipated.

Octavian took the name Gaius Julius Caesar, and quickly curried favor with the army by paying bo-

She was splendid to hear and to see, and was capable of conquering the hearts which had resisted most obstinately the influence of love and those which had been frozen by age.
—DIO CASSIUS
Roman historian,
on Cleopatra

Isis, the Egyptian goddess of fertility, is portrayed in the painting on the left with Nefertari, a 13th-century B.C. queen. In the same headdress, which symbolizes the moon, the figure representing the goddess in the sculpture here is said to be Cleopatra.

nuses to Caesar's troops. He also found allies among Antony's enemies in Rome, among them the celebrated Cicero, who wrote a series of denunciations against Antony, accusing him of dishonesty and unfitness for leadership.

It was not long before Antony had to come to terms with Octavian. Together with Lepidus, the three men formed what was called the second triumvirate. They had, for the present, the goal of pursuing and punishing Caesar's assassins. No one doubted, however, that eventually Antony's and Octavian's ambitions would bring them into conflict.

In 42 B.C., on the fields of Philippi in Greece, the triumvirate's forces defeated the army that Brutus and Cassius had raised. Since Octavian had fallen seriously ill during the battle, most of the glory fell directly on Antony's shoulders.

With some justification, Antony now felt himself to be the unchallenged leader of the Roman Empire. Taking up Caesar's plans for an invasion of Parthia, he brought his army to Greece, and then on to Asia in the eastern Mediterranean.

In the city of Ephesus, Antony's popularity was demonstrated by his reception as the new Dionysus (the Greek god of fertility and wine). He was met at the gate by a procession of women dressed as the handmaidens of Dionysus, and men and boys costumed as the mythological satyrs and fauns that were often associated with Dionysus. His popularity diminished somewhat when it became known that he was levying a tax on the citizens to support his invasion of Parthia, but no one dared to openly oppose him.

Soon after, he was to make the fateful request that Cleopatra meet him in Tarsus. He wanted her to answer a charge that she had helped the conspirators in their fight against the second triumvirate.

From Tarsus, Antony sent a messenger who bade Cleopatra to appear "in her best attire," hardly a necessary instruction for the Egyptian queen. Cleopatra knew quite a bit about Antony. He had been a frequent guest of Caesar's while she was living in Rome. In addition, there was a considerable amount of gossip about this important man. She knew how

A celebrated hostess, Cleopatra entertained Antony with a lavish hand. Here, preparing a royal feast, servants head for the palace kitchen with nets full of seafood, platters of fish, baskets of eggs, jugs of wine, and animals for the butchers, who are pictured slaughtering a cow.

helpful he could be for her, and how useful she and her country could be for him. But she also knew how much more he would want to see her if she kept him waiting, so she ignored the summons. A second one came, and then a third, but she didn't respond.

Cleopatra had confidence in her power to allure. As Plutarch says, "She brought with her her surest hopes in her own magic weapons and charms." In truth, Cleopatra must have compared herself favorably with the women she had seen in Rome. Part of her "magic" charms were the makeup secrets that she had learned as a young woman in Alexandria — rouges, eyeshadows, and lip colorings were all products of Egypt. Purportedly she even wrote a book detailing makeup techniques and other measures by which women could attract men.

She was about 28 years old when she captivated Antony in Tarsus. According to Plutarch, "The last and crowning mischief that could befall [Antony] came in the love of Cleopatra. It awakened and kindled to fury passions that as yet lay still and dormant in his nature, and to stifle and finally corrupt any elements that yet made resistance in him of goodness and a sound judgment. He fell into the snare."

After their meeting in Tarsus, Antony set about consolidating the outposts of the Roman Empire in Asia. He confirmed Cleopatra as ruler of Egypt and conferred Cyprus on her as well. This was not quite enough for her; she also wanted the death of the last of her siblings, her younger sister Arsinoë.

After Caesar's Triumph, Arsinoë had found asylum in the temple of Artemis in Ephesus. At Antony's order, she was taken from the refuge and murdered. Cleopatra was now the only one of Auletes's children alive, the only person with a legitimate claim to Egypt's throne.

Antony also named a ruler for Syria and Judea (modern-day Israel). Herod the Great, who is mentioned in the Bible as the ruler of Judea at the time Jesus Christ was born, and who was to become Cleopatra's bitter enemy, was confirmed as Judea's king. Antony took this action because Parthian troops, led by a renegade Roman, were poised on the Syrian frontier. He wanted to ensure that the

There's not a minute of our lives should stretch Without some pleasure now. What sport tonight?

—Marc Antony, from William Shakespeare's play *Antony and Cleopatra*

border areas under Roman rule were led by people loyal to him. Having accomplished this, he decided to accept Cleopatra's invitation to visit Alexandria.

In Alexandria, Cleopatra displayed the sophisticated delights of the city to a suitably impressed Antony. They socialized with a group of rich and pleasure-seeking friends who called themselves "The Order of Those Who Live for Pleasure." The privileged members of this "club" vied with each other in staging lavish entertainments, although no one surpassed Cleopatra.

It is said that the kitchen staff at the palace was ready at all times to produce a feast for Cleopatra and her guests. On one occasion, a visitor entered the kitchen and saw eight wild boars waiting to be roasted. The visitor asked if Cleopatra was having a banquet that night. The head cook laughed and said that there would only be a small group that night but, since they never knew quite when a meal would be desired, they had to cook continuously. Only at a certain stage is a roast fit to eat.

The Egyptian queen anticipated Antony's every wish. "At any moment," says Plutarch, "she had some new delight or charm to meet his wishes; at every turn she was upon him, and let him escape her neither by day nor night. She played at dice with him, drank with him, hunted with him."

For amusement, Cleopatra and Antony would sometimes get quite drunk, dress in servants' clothes and go about the city at night rapping on people's doors and windows and playing jokes on them. Occasionally, Antony would get into fights with people who resented this interruption of their sleep. But most people guessed who their visitors were.

This was probably not an entertainment in which Cleopatra normally indulged, but she perceived that it was just the sort of thing that Antony enjoyed. As word of these antics got around, the Alexandrians began to regard Antony as a childlike figure under the spell of Cleopatra. According to a popular saying, Antony reserved his tragic roles for Rome, and played only comedy in Alexandria.

One popular story concerned a fishing trip the

Her delightful way of speaking was such that she captured all who listened to her.
—DIO CASSIUS
Roman historian,
on Cleopatra

lovers took. Antony was unable to catch anything, and bribed a servant to dive under the water and attach fish to his hook. When he began to pull in one fish after another, Cleopatra caught on. The next day, she had a diver put a stiff, salted fish on Antony's hook. When Antony lifted his "catch" into the boat, there was great laughter among the guests. Cleopatra told Antony, "Leave the fishing-rod, General, to us poor sovereigns of Pharos and Canopus; your game is cities, provinces, and king-doms." It was shrewd advice. Cleopatra knew that if Antony was to remain ruler of the empire, he would have to attain some military victories.

Antony was thinking along the same lines. He was not just in Egypt to enjoy himself with Cleopatra; he needed Egypt's huge wealth for his planned war against the Parthians. He wanted Alexandria as a supply base, and was relying on Egypt's shipbuild-ing capacity in case of a naval war against Octavian.

Cleopatra, on the other hand, longed to restore the former glories of her country. She wanted to extend its frontiers to where they had been in the early days of the Ptolemies. She needed Roman sup-port to realize these dreams. With it, she might yet see Alexandria rise to become the capital of an em-pire as great as Alexander's.

Events elsewhere did not stand still while Antony was enjoying himself with Cleopatra. The Parthians launched an attack against Syria and Asia Minor. Antony also learned that his wife and brother were battling a recovered Octavian in Rome. Antony real-ized that the time for celebration was past; it was time to take action. As he was setting out for the Parthian frontier, he heard that his wife and brother had been defeated by Octavian. He immediately changed course and headed for Rome.

Antony's wife Fulvia was an ambitious woman. Her character sheds some light on Antony's rela-tionship with Cleopatra. As described by Plutarch, Fulvia was "a woman not born for spinning nor housewifery, nor one that could be content with ruling a private husband, but prepared to govern a first magistrate, or give orders to a commander in chief. Cleopatra was obliged to her for having taught

Antony to be so good a servant. He came to her hands tame and broken into entire obedience to the commands of a mistress."

As it happened, Fulvia soon died and Antony was thus able to patch up an agreement with Octavian. The two of them met at Brundisium, in southern Italy, in 40 B.C. and made a formal division of the empire among the members of the triumvirate. With the Ionian Sea as the dividing line, Antony got the eastern part, Octavian the western, and Lepidus was given the provinces in Africa. To cement the

Like Dionysus, the Greek god of wine and fertility with whom he was often identified, Antony enjoyed the fruits of the vine, as had the ancient Egyptians. This 3,000-year-old painting depicts vineyard workers picking grapes for Egypt's royal winery.

agreement, Antony agreed to marry Octavian's half-sister Octavia.

Such marriages between the families of political rivals were common in Rome. It is doubtful that the celebration of Antony's marriage to Octavia meant a disavowal of his feelings toward Cleopatra. It merely showed that Antony was aware of political realities. He was not prepared, as Caesar had been, to flout public opinion in Rome by bringing his Egyptian mistress home.

Next, Antony sent a trusted general to forestall the Parthian advance in the eastern provinces while Antony and Octavian began three years of jockeying for position in Rome. Octavia seems to have been a dutiful wife, but it was said that Antony never trusted her, seeing her as a spy for her brother.

Antony's main concern at this time was in raising troops and supplies for a major assault against Parthia. Of the three Roman triumvirs, Antony was regarded as the best military leader. He felt that an important victory would erase the stain of the earlier defeat which forced him to share power with Octavian and Lepidus, and increase his leverage over Octavian.

It was said that Antony chafed at not being able to politically outmaneuver this youthful upstart. An Egyptian soothsayer in Rome is said to have warned Antony, "Though the fortune that attends you is bright and glorious, yet it is overshadowed by Octavian's." The soothsayer advised Antony to keep his distance from Octavian, "for your spirit dreads his; when absent from him, yours is proud and brave, but in his presence it is unmanly and dejected." The soothsayer may have in fact been acting on Cleopatra's orders, trying to persuade Antony to leave Rome and return to Alexandria. As it developed, however, the advice was sound.

Cleopatra must have been hurt and angered upon hearing of Antony's marriage. It probably seemed that her own hopes for an alliance were dashed. In the year following Antony's departure from Alexandria, Cleopatra had given birth to twins, Alexander Helios and Cleopatra Selene. Their ambitious mother kept a careful eye on Roman politics through

It is easy to follow propaganda and legend and see Antony hopelessly seduced and subservient to a sensuous foreign queen. Passion not withstanding, however, both pursued rational political interests. Each had something to gain by cooperating with the other—Cleopatra the support of Roman arms against her rivals, Antony Egyptian wealth to defray the costs of a projected war against Parthia and rivalry with Octavia.
—FRITZ M. HEICHELHEIM
modern historian

agents such as the soothsayer who advised Antony.

Antony finally readied his forces for the Parthian campaign. He took his wife Octavia with him as far as Greece. He then proceeded to Antioch, Syria, sending a message to Cleopatra to meet him there.

The two had been separated for more than three years. Yet, as Plutarch says, "The mischief that had long lain still, that passion for Cleopatra which better thoughts had seemed to lull and charm into oblivion, now gathered strength again . . . and broke out into a flame."

Antioch, a beautiful city on the Orontes River, had been the capital of the Seleucid Empire. Shortly after Cleopatra's arrival there in 37 B.C., Antony seems to have gone through a marriage ceremony with her. The marriage was not, of course, recognized in Rome, but was accepted in Egypt and the eastern parts of the empire.

Antony bestowed on Cleopatra much of the empire that had been held by the early Ptolemies. He also recognized her twin children as his son and daughter. Finally, he gave Cleopatra numerous titles and crowns — honors designed to increase her prestige.

After wintering in Antioch with Cleopatra, Antony launched his Parthian campaign in the spring of 36 B.C. He adopted Caesar's plan of going through Armenia to attack from the northeast. As he crossed the Parthian border, he commanded what was probably the largest Roman army assembled up to that time. It included 60,000 legionaries and 10,000 horsemen from Gaul and Spain.

But Antony lacked Caesar's military genius. He had not adequately secured Armenia and had unwisely fragmented his army. He went ahead with faster troops and cavalry, leaving behind the heavy siege equipment that would be sorely needed later. Plutarch says that Antony rushed ahead because he wanted desperately to get back to Cleopatra: "It was as if he were no longer the master of his own judgment, but rather under the influence of some drug or magic spell for he gave the impression that his eyes were constantly drawn to her image and his thoughts fixed upon hastening his return rather

It is not that Antony did not care for [Octavia]. He was not inhuman, but he was even more concerned with challenging her brother for supremacy in the Roman world, and Cleopatra had more to offer in achieving that goal than Octavia could.
—FRITZ M. HEICHELHEIM
modern historian

than upon conquering the enemy."

Antony trusted the Armenian king to supply additional cavalry and protect his rear guard. Instead, the king permitted the Parthians to circle behind Antony. They destroyed 300 Roman wagons along with their siege engines, as well as two legions. Their golden eagles were added to those captured at Carrhae in 53 B.C., when Crassus had suffered one of Rome's worst military defeats in history.

Antony proceeded with his main force until he reached the Parthian summer capital at Phraaspa. However, he could not breach the city wall without his battering rams and siege engines. Though he held the area around the capital, he could not obtain enough supplies to feed his army. He had no choice but to retreat.

After the siege 5,000 of Antony's wounded were carried to a spot outside his camp. Antony, it is said,

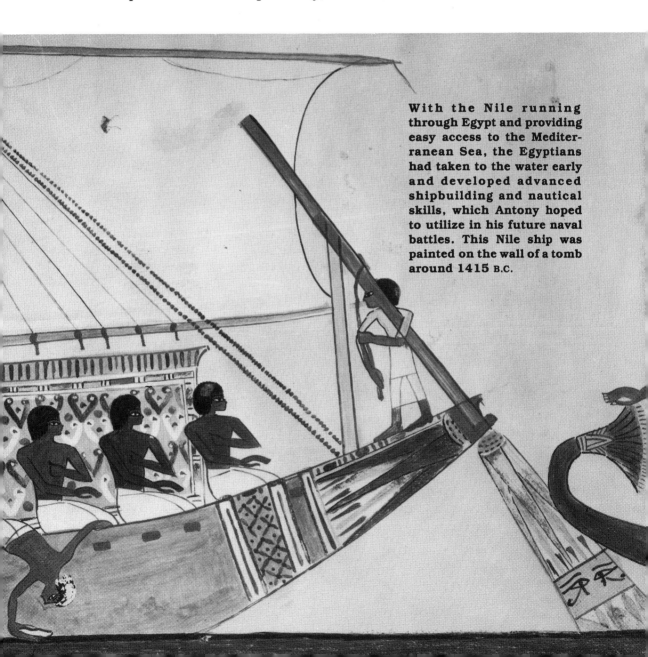

With the Nile running through Egypt and providing easy access to the Mediterranean Sea, the Egyptians had taken to the water early and developed advanced shipbuilding and nautical skills, which Antony hoped to utilize in his future naval battles. This Nile ship was painted on the wall of a tomb around 1415 B.C.

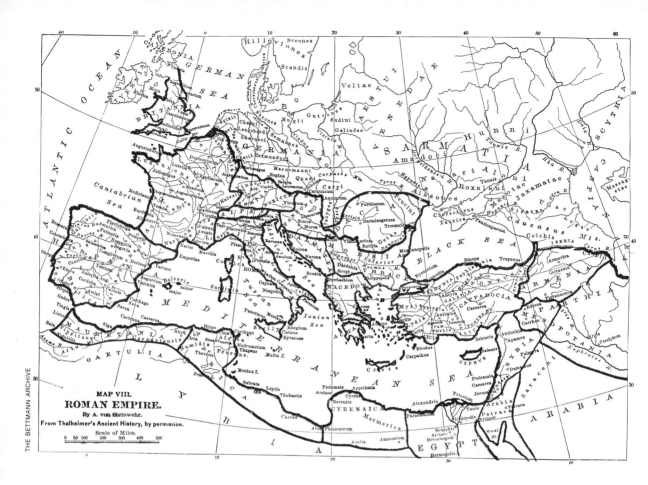

MAP VIII.
ROMAN EMPIRE.
By A. von Steinwehr.
From Thalheimer's Ancient History, by permission.
Scale of Miles.
0 50 100   200   300   400   500

From Italy, the Romans set forth to conquer the known world. When Antony and Octavian ruled as members of the second triumvirate (43–28 B.C.), the Roman Empire included much of Europe, North Africa, and the Middle East. This map shows the extent of the Roman Empire at its height two centuries after the death of Cleopatra.

"went from tent to tent to visit and comfort them, and was not able to see his men without tears and a passion of grief."

The retreat was skillfully accomplished. There were even a few successful actions carried out en route. Plutarch describes how on one occasion the Romans formed the famous *testudo* (tortoise) to protect themselves against the Parthians during an attack: "The shield-bearers wheeled about, enclosing the lighter armed troops within their ranks while they themselves dropped on one knee and held their shields out in front of them. The second rank held their shields over the head of the first, and the next rank likewise. This tactic produces a most striking appearance, rather like the roof of a house, and it is very effective against arrows, which merely skim off it. The Parthians, however, seeing the Romans dropping on one knee, thought that they were exhausted, so they laid down their bows and came in at close quarters with their spears. Then the Romans suddenly sprang up, giving a battle cry, and killed the foremost of the enemy with their javelins, and put the rest to rout."

Despite his several successes, Antony suffered an important defeat and lost many men who would be needed later for a final battle with Octavian. In Asia, and more importantly, in Rome, the defeat caused Antony a loss of prestige.

Meanwhile, Cleopatra had made her way back to Alexandria. She stopped to meet Herod, who was — by Antony's decree — the ruler of the only portions of the old Ptolemaic empire that were still not in Cleopatra's hands. Though Cleopatra continually pleaded with Antony for Herod's kingdom, he never gave it to her. Antony needed the strong military support that Herod could provide.

The meeting between Herod and Cleopatra was unpleasant. Some historians report that he attempted to have her killed while she was in his capital. This is unlikely, because Herod would have feared Antony's angry reprisal.

Cleopatra returned to Alexandria, and gave birth to a son named Ptolemy Philadelphus, after Ptolemy II, under whom the Ptolemaic empire had reached its height. She must have awaited the news of Antony's campaign nervously.

According to legend, the twins Romulus and Remus were fathered by Mars, the god of war, were abandoned as babies, and raised by a wolf. Romulus lived to become a king and founded the city of Rome.

The catapult was introduced as a weapon of war around 400 B.C. It was designed to throw stones and other heavy missiles, as well as arrows, and was capable of breaking walls. Having lost the catapults he needed to storm the capital of Parthia, Marc Antony was defeated in his eastern campaign and several thousand Roman soldiers died.

At last a message arrived, calling on her to bring money and supplies to Antony's troops. The news of his retreat must have been a blow; Cleopatra had always said that Antony's main enemy was Octavian, not the Parthians. Nevertheless, she raised supplies and money for Antony's troops.

We can see from this action how the relationship between the two benefited both politically. Even if their love had not been a factor, Cleopatra was still a client-ruler of Antony's in the East, as Herod and other rulers were. In return for his support and bequests, she was expected to assist his military adventures.

Antony returned to Alexandria, where he and Cleopatra began planning a new campaign. They resumed their high style of living, and it was reported that Antony began drinking heavily. While there he received a message from Octavia, saying that she was going to Athens with troops and supplies for her husband.

It seems that it was Octavian who encouraged Octavia to go to Greece. Plutarch describes his motive: "It is generally agreed that Octavian allowed her to do this not so much to give her pleasure, but rather to give himself a plausible pretext for declaring war, if she were neglected or insulted by her husband." Antony probably realized it was his last chance to reach a peaceful solution to his rivalry with Octavian. According to Plutarch, he considered responding to his wife's offer, but Cleopatra was determined to keep Antony with her. "So she pretended to be dying for love of Antony, bringing her body down by diet. When he entered the room, she fixed her eyes upon him in a rapture, and when he left, seemed to languish and half faint away. She took great pains that he should see her in tears, and, as soon as he noticed it, hastily dried them up and turned away, as if she wished that he should know nothing of it."

This sounds melodramatic, but we must remember that Plutarch was writing after the fact and was a historian in the empire ruled by Octavian's successors. It was not uncommon for rulers to destroy records that described their adversaries in a positive light. In any case, we know that Antony took the supplies and troops but refused to see Octavia. She returned to Rome, where her brother was suitably angered by Antony's treatment of her.

In 34 B.C. Antony attacked the kingdom of Armenia in revenge for the king's treachery during the Parthian campaign. Antony brought the king and his family back to Alexandria as prisoners.

Though this was really a rather minor victory, Antony held a Triumph for himself in Alexandria. The Armenian king was marched in golden chains through the streets to Cleopatra's feet. This was a break with Roman tradition. Triumphs were for

Preparing to conquer Parthia, Marc Antony made a serious tactical error. Leaving most of his troops and heavy weapons behind, he rushed ahead with his cavalry. This cameo depicts a lone Roman horseman engaged in battle.

Rome — no Roman had ever celebrated one anywhere else. To the people of Rome, Antony's Alexandrian Triumph was tantamount to placing Cleopatra's capital on an equal basis with Rome.

But this was a minor affair compared with what came next. Antony held a great feast for the people of Alexandria. It was a scene of oriental splendor, more typical of Cleopatra's planning than Antony's. High above the crowd sat Antony and Cleopatra on golden thrones set atop a platform of silver.

Cleopatra was dressed as the goddess Isis. Antony was dressed not as a Roman, but as the Greek god Dionysus. Statues at the feast showed Antony as both Osiris and Dionysus. Below them sat the four children Cleopatra had borne, dressed in the costumes of various countries of Asia and the eastern Mediterranean. The reason soon became clear.

Antony proclaimed Cleopatra the co-ruler with Caesarion of Egypt, Cyprus, Libya, and Syria. He recognized Caesarion as the true son of Caesar, a calculated slap at Octavian.

Antony also gave the rule of Armenia, Media (the northwest area of modern Iran), and Parthia to his and Cleopatra's son Alexander — anticipating the conquest of Parthia. To his son Ptolemy Philadelphus, Antony gave Phoenicia, parts of Syria, and Cilicia (modern-day southeastern Turkey). Their daughter, Cleopatra Selene, received Cyrenaica and Libya in Africa. The children were dressed in the costumes of the lands they were destined to rule.

Cleopatra was given the title Queen of Kings, and her son Caesarion proclaimed King of Kings. Antony had another son, named Antylus, by Fulvia. To him he gave the western parts of the empire, signifying Antony's intention to take these from Octavian.

Cleopatra, Antony, and their children would thus jointly rule an area larger than that of Alexander's empire — stretching from India to the Atlantic, from the English Channel to the Sahara Desert and the Indian Ocean. Cleopatra had attained the honor and power she yearned for even if her rule was over an empire yet to be conquered. And she planned to use Antony's generalship and her own resources to truly become the Queen of Kings.

> *Age cannot wither her, nor*
> *custom stale*
> *Her infinite variety: other*
> *women cloy*
> *The appetites they feed, but*
> *she makes hungry*
> *Where most she satisfies.*
> —WILLIAM SHAKESPEARE
> poet and dramatist,
> describing Cleopatra in
> his play *Antony*
> *and Cleopatra*

In a gala celebration in Alexandria, Antony bestowed various sections of the Roman Empire on the queen of Egypt and her children. While Cleopatra dressed as Isis (left), Antony was portrayed in statues representing Isis's husband, Osiris, the Egyptian god of death and rebirth.

4

The Challenge to Rome

The grand ceremony in which Antony bestowed the rule of a good part of the Roman Empire on Cleopatra and her children — called the Donations of Alexandria — was certain to have political repercussions in Rome. By this time, Lepidus, the third member of the second triumvirate, had been defeated by Octavian, and the battle lines between Antony and Octavian were clearly drawn.

Both sides immediately began maneuvering to improve their positions. Cleopatra's and Antony's son Alexander Helios was promised in marriage to the daughter of the King of Media, thus gaining another ally for Antony. Similarly, Antony requested and received renewed pledges of support from his client-kings in the eastern Mediterranean.

For his part Octavian began trying to fan public opposition to Antony in Rome. He accused him of driving a wedge between the eastern provinces and Rome, and repeatedly drew attention to Antony's obvious infidelity to Octavia. In response, Antony sent a rather coarse letter to Octavian asking if *his* wife were the only woman he took as a lover, and then named some prominent women of Rome as likely lovers of Octavian. He also accused Octavian

GIRAUDON/ART RESOURCE

A Roman coin bearing Marc Antony's profile, issued in 41 B.C. Eight years later he requested Cleopatra's financial assistance to purchase the military equipment he would need to overcome Octavian.

A sculpture of the Praetorian Guards, those men charged with the safety of Rome's ruler. Shocked by reports of Antony's plans for carving up the Roman Empire, Romans were further scandalized by rumors that his bodyguards carried shields displaying Cleopatra's name.

ART RESOURCE

87

The goddess Roma leads the Roman army into battle. Though Antony's men admired him as a military commander, they detested Cleopatra's influence over him and her insistence on participating in military planning. The Roman troops also feared they might be obliged to pay homage to the queen of Egypt, a disquieting idea to loyal Roman legionaries.

of failing to share with him the part of the empire that Lepidus had formerly controlled.

These interchanges took place in 33 B.C. while Antony was in Armenia shoring up alliances. The formal compact between Antony and Octavian was due to expire at the end of the year. It had been previously agreed that two of Antony's supporters would be the consuls of Rome for 32 B.C., and that Antony and Octavian would share the consulship the following year.

Cleopatra and Antony spent the winter in Ephesus. They began to assemble ships and legions from all over their domain. Cleopatra contributed a huge amount of money and agreed to provision the army during the war. She also contributed 200 ships to Antony's total fleet of 800.

The physical presence of Cleopatra among the forces preparing for war did little to enhance Antony's cause. As some of his advisers were quick to point out, her presence had hurt troop morale and had even triggered some desertions. As a result, Antony asked Cleopatra to return to Egypt. But she feared that without her there to shore up his resolve, Antony might become reconciled with Octavia. She persuaded a Roman adviser, Canidius, to argue her case with Antony.

Canidius said that "one who had played such an important role in assembling the forces should not be robbed of her share of the glory in carrying on the campaign." In addition, repudiating Cleopatra might anger the Egyptians who comprised a significant part of Antony's naval forces. The final point that Canidius made was that he could see no indication that Cleopatra was inferior in intelligence to any of the kings who were taking part in the expedition.

Predictably, Antony gave in and allowed Cleopatra to remain. No one can say how much his love for her influenced his decision. Certainly the political considerations argued by Canidius were not without some merit. Yet Cleopatra's continued presence would prove disastrous in the end.

In Rome, Octavian continued to hammer away on the Cleopatra issue. Some of Antony's officers had deserted him and returned to Rome, claiming that Cleopatra had insulted them. They also told Octavian that Antony had deposited his will with the Vestals (the high priestesses) in Rome. Upon hearing this, Octavian had the will seized and publicly read what he regarded as incriminating portions of it. In it Antony asked to have his body carried through the Forum and then sent to Cleopatra for burial in Alexandria. Most Roman citizens thought it unthinkable that a Roman would not want burial on Roman soil.

Octavian pressed the attack, appealing to Roman pride by arguing that if Antony became ruler of the empire, Rome would take second place to Alexandria. Octavian's supporters also spread rumors about the scandalous hold that Cleopatra apparently had over her Roman lover. It was said that at a state banquet Antony had gone so far as to massage Cleopatra's feet in front of shocked guests.

Another widely circulated rumor was that Antony, even while holding public audiences with the kings and princes of his realm, would regularly receive love notes from Cleopatra. Supposedly, on such occasions he would ignore the business at hand and openly read the notes without embarrassment.

Another time, Furnius, a Roman lawyer of great authority and eloquence, was pleading a case before Antony. When Cleopatra happened to pass by, Antony allegedly rose in the middle of Furnius's speech and followed Cleopatra like the most docile servant.

Patriotic Romans listened to such stories with increasing disgust and bewilderment. Was this the way for a powerful Roman to act? And every day there seemed to be a new story tailor-made for ridicule. Antony had deserted Roman ways; Antony wore an Egyptian dagger at his belt; Antony walked while Cleopatra was carried on a palanquin, or sedan chair; Antony had Cleopatra's name embossed on the shields of his Roman bodyguards. Whether true or not, the steady stream of such reports convinced many that Cleopatra was a threat to Rome.

Much of this was undoubtedly false. It is hard to separate fact from fiction, or to determine Antony's real intentions, because after Octavian became em-

[Cleopatra,] intoxicated with hopes and the delirium of exalted fortune, dreams of the fall of the Capitol and the funeral of the Empire.

—OCTAVIAN
Roman statesman, later
Emperor Augustus

peror, all the historical accounts favoring Antony were destroyed. Thus we see Antony and Cleopatra only through highly prejudicial eyes.

In Rome, a very real crisis erupted when the two Antony supporters became consuls in 32 B.C. On their first day in office they denounced Octavian (who was not present) before the Senate and called for his censure. The Senate refused to act on their proposal, and a couple days later Octavian formally replied, promising to show proof of Antony's misdeeds.

The temper of Rome was now decidedly with Octavian, and shortly afterward the two consuls and about 400 of the 1,200 senators fled the city to join Cleopatra and Antony in Ephesus. Later in the year Antony made a final break by formally divorcing Octavia. This eroded his support in Rome even further, for Octavia had always been steadfastly faithful to him. She cared for his children by Fulvia as well as the children she and Antony had together. Now Antony told her to take her children and leave his house in Rome.

Octavian responded by declaring war. Cleverly, he declared it on Cleopatra, calling Antony the agent of a foreign state. Both sides now began to draw their forces together for a decisive battle.

Cleopatra and Antony sailed to the island of Samos, off Greece, where they held a great festival. All their allies in the East were summoned there, and the actors, singers, musicians, and entertainers of the area were assembled. The island "for some days resounded with piping and harping, theaters filling, and choruses playing. Every city sent an ox as its contribution . . . and the kings who accompanied Antony competed at making the most magnificent feasts and the greatest presents. Men began to ask themselves, what would be done to celebrate the victory, when they went to such an expense of festivity at the opening of the war." The answer to that would never be known.

The premature triumphal celebration then proceeded to Athens, where Antony had honored Octavia some years before. Cleopatra now received even greater honors. Sports events and plays were

She fought like a tigress for her child by Caesar, and her children by Antony. A large part of her life may be seen as a struggle to try to ensure that her children should inherit her empire and her throne. Nothing should be allowed to stand in her way if their interests were threatened.
—ERNLE BRADFORD
modern historian,
on Cleopatra

The Atrium, or central hall, of the Vestals, the six priestesses whose major duty was to keep the sacred fire burning in the temple of Vesta, the Roman goddess of the
hearth. Expressing the wish to be buried in Egypt, Antony
left his will in their keeping.

staged for her pleasure. Special deputations of Athenians visited her house with lavish gifts.

Antony and Cleopatra did have good reason to believe that victory lay at hand. Antony controlled the richest part of the empire, territory stretching from the Euphrates River to the Ionian Sea. Also, Antony still regarded Octavian with contempt, and had repeatedly accused him of cowardice at the Battle of Philippi. Older and more experienced in battle, Antony still saw Octavian as a mere upstart who had claimed Caesar's legacy as an 18-year-old student from Greece.

But the years had changed both men. While Antony was frittering his time away with Cleopatra and waging a lackluster campaign against Parthia, Octavian had built his power. Though his part of the empire did not have the riches of the East, it was the source of most of Rome's military manpower.

Octavian also proved to be a good judge of men. Knowing that Antony was a better general than he, Octavian put Marcus Agrippa in command of his forces. Agrippa had successfully waged battles against the pirates of Sicily. In him, Octavian found a military commander at least the equal of Antony.

During the summer of 32 B.C., Antony moved his army overland to Greece to join the navy that was already assembled there. Caesar, in Antony's place, would no doubt have chosen to take the battle to Octavian and invade Italy. Antony could not do this, because to land in Italy with Cleopatra would have aroused fierce opposition from every Roman. And she would not let him go to Italy without her.

In early 31 B.C., Octavian crossed the Adriatic Sea. He established a camp north of Actium on the Northwestern coast of Greece. Antony's land forces assembled south of Actium, while his fleet was anchored at the nearby Gulf of Ambracia.

Antony had about 500 warships in the gulf, including decorated war galleys propelled by eight to ten banks of oars. Plutarch estimates that he had 100,000 foot soldiers and 12,000 cavalry.

Octavian's forces were less — about 250 war galleys, 80,000 foot soldiers, and 12,000 cavalry. But Agrippa scored a significant victory by capturing

> *Cleopatra was capable of ruthlessness and even murder in defense of her throne and her kingdom, but her actions were as nothing compared with those of the Roman leaders who were fighting among themselves for the mastery of the world.*
> —ERNLE BRADFORD
> modern historian

parts of the Greek coast to the south, a move which cut off Antony's supply lines. He now had to bring supplies overland through a more difficult route.

Antony seemed to be trapped in a harbor that he himself had picked. His generals urged him to withdraw the army to central Greece. Cleopatra vetoed the plan, because this would have meant abandoning the fleet at Actium and leaving Egypt open to invasion by sea.

When Antony yielded to Cleopatra, several of his most important officers deserted. As the desertions continued, Antony began executing those caught trying to escape to Octavian's side.

The Battle of Actium was a sea battle. Antony decided to take his ships through the blockade that Octavian had established at the entrance to the strait. Antony's army was supposed to march overland to Asia Minor to link up with the naval forces later.

Many historians have criticized this decision, and it is not known just what Antony's real objectives were. Did he intend to engage Octavian's fleet and destroy it? Or was this merely an attempt to get past the blockade and save the fleet for a future battle?

The conventional wisdom is that since Antony's land forces were superior to Octavian's, he should have waged a land battle. It was only from "obedience to his mistress that he wished the victory to be gained by sea." According to Plutarch, Antony's ships were undermanned and "his captains, all through unhappy Greece, were pressing [forcibly inducting] every description of men, common travelers and ass-drivers, harvest workers, and boys, and even so the vessels . . . remained, most of them, ill-manned and badly rowed."

Ships meant for a sea battle outside the harbor would be powered by banks of rowers; it was only for long voyages that sails were needed. Yet Antony ordered that sails be taken aboard the ships. The treasury they had accumulated was placed on board Cleopatra's flagship. Confident as Antony and Cleopatra were, it appears they were still pragmatic enough to consider the possibility that they might need to flee.

THE METROPOLITAN MUSEUM OF ART, BEQUEST OF WALTER C. BAKER, 1971

Combining the ideals of Greece with those of the Middle East, this Grecian statuette is said to come from Alexandria, where Antony reveled with Cleopatra while Octavian was building a mighty military force.

Recognizing his own inexperience as a military leader, Octavian placed his army under the command of Marcus Agrippa, a general noted for his naval skills. Although his men were outnumbered by Antony's, Agrippa won a foothold on the southern coast of Greece, cutting off Antony's major supply route.

Cleopatra took the initiative in flight; Antony chose to be the companion of the fleeing queen rather than of his fighting soldiers, and the commander, whose duty it would have been to deal severely with deserters, now became a deserter from his own army.

—VELLEIUS
Roman historian

In those days ships attacked with battering rams set in front of the prow. Antony's ships also had brass spikes along the sides to protect them from being rammed. Towers constructed at bow and stern held soldiers who shot arrows and flung rocks and flaming objects aboard enemy ships. Many hearts must have beat faster on both sides as Antony's ships appeared in a long line, making fast for Octavian's fleet.

Marcus Agrippa, commanding Octavian's naval forces, at first ordered his ships to draw back. This was not a retreat, but a maneuver to spread Antony's ships out from their tight formation.

The moment came. The lines of ships met, and the men aboard began raining death upon the crews of the other side.

The battle lasted only a few minutes. After the first engagement, Cleopatra's flagship and the 60 Egyptian ships that were part of the attacking fleet raised their sails and headed for the open sea. They were running.

The effect on the rest of Antony's forces can easily be imagined. But the worst came when Antony set sail after Cleopatra, earning for himself the contempt of nearly all who wrote of the battle afterward.

Plutarch spared no venom: "Here it was that Antony showed to all the world that he was no longer actuated by the thoughts and motives of a commander or a man, or indeed by his own judgment. What was once said as a jest — that the soul of a lover lives in someone else's body — he proved to be a serious truth. For, as if he had been born part of her, and must move with her wherever she went, as soon as he saw her ship sailing away, he abandoned all who were fighting and spending their lives for him. . . . He followed her that had so well begun his ruin and hereafter accomplished it."

Antony had taken a small, fast galley to catch up with Cleopatra. Seeing him approach, she gave the signal to take him aboard. Their cause was lost but at least they would be together.

Depicted in a sculptural relief, a Roman warship carries troops to battle. Antony's officers in Greece advised him to fight on land, but Cleopatra, fearing that Octavian's fleet might attack Egypt, convinced Antony to engage in a naval battle.

5

The Last Year

When Antony was taken aboard Cleopatra's flagship, he was a broken man. He sat alone and silent at the ship's prow, covering his face with his hands. There he remained for three days, until the ship touched land at the southern tip of the Greek peninsula. According to Plutarch, "it was here that Cleopatra's waiting women first persuaded the two to speak to one another and then later to eat and sleep together." They were soon joined by other ships that had escaped from Actium, bringing news of the total defeat of the rest of the fleet. Then Antony took a merchant ship to the North African coast west of Egypt, where he hoped to find safety and support.

Cleopatra took the remnants of the fleet on to Egypt. Twice she had gambled on a man who could help her restore the glories of the Ptolemies. Twice she had lost. But Cleopatra was not one to give up. She had greater resolve than Antony, and was already making plans as she sailed into the Great Harbor at Alexandria with sails high.

The news of Antony's defeat might have given her enemies at home ideas about overthrowing her to curry favor with Octavian. She knew how quickly political loyalties could switch and promptly made

Cleopatra's profile appears on this ancient coin, with her name inscribed in Greek. Even as she fled from Actium, Cleopatra planned her escape, trusting that her fortune would assure her refuge somewhere in Asia.

After his decisive victory over Antony and Cleopatra at Actium, Octavian was well on his way to assuming sole leadership of Rome. In 27 B.C. Octavian would accept the honorific title "Augustus" (revered), and eventually establish an imperial dynasty, thus destroying the last vestiges of republican democracy — as many Romans had once feared Julius Caesar would.

arrangements to forestall any immediate opposition. Since Cleopatra had the army aboard her ships, she lost no time in consolidating her authority in the city.

She devised a grand plan to move her fleet across land. At that time there was no Suez Canal to connect the Mediterranean with the Red Sea. (The early Ptolemies had, in fact, constructed such a canal, but centuries of neglect had caused it to silt over.) Cleopatra planned to drag her ships across the narrow neck of land that would take them into the Red Sea. From there she could sail to any place in Asia, where she had good relations with many of Egypt's trading partners. She hoped that her soldiers and treasure would secure her a warm welcome.

However, now that Octavian had won the decisive victory over Antony, allies flocked to his side. The Arabians of Petra (part of modern-day Jordan) attacked and destroyed the Egyptian fleet, undoubtedly with Octavian's backing.

Meanwhile, Antony received more crushing news. The man whom he had put in charge of his forces in Africa had deserted to Octavian. Antony considered killing himself, an honorable end for Romans defeated in battle. But friends convinced him that a future victory was still possible.

Having no place else to go, Antony sailed to the island of Pharos near Alexandria. There he tried to seal himself off from the world, but he could not avoid the messengers who brought him discouraging news. The troops he had left at Actium had surrendered to Octavian. In addition, the kings and princes in his eastern provinces, including Herod, had sworn their loyalty to the new ruler of Rome.

The extensive empire that Antony and Cleopatra had so recently controlled had now shrunk to Egypt alone. Cleopatra ordered the fortification of all approaches to Egypt; no doubt Octavian had plans for the Egyptians as well. Finding no solace on Pharos, Antony soon joined Cleopatra at her palace. During the last winter of their lives, they returned once again to festivals, celebrations, and pleasure. The teenagers Caesarion and Antylus, Antony's son by Fulvia, received the *toga virilis*, a Roman garment

which symbolized a young man's coming of age. Alexandria celebrated the event for many days.

The old group that had called itself "The Order of Those Who Live for Pleasure" had broken up. In its place Antony and Cleopatra established a new group, which all those willing to die together in Alexandria were invited to join. The new group was called, quite appropriately as events transpired, "The Order of Those Inseparable in Death."

Meanwhile, Cleopatra collected various kinds of deadly poisons. She tested them on prisoners who had been condemned to death, in order to discern which was the most painless. When she found that

Together again in Alexandria, Antony and Cleopatra gathered their friends to resume the life they had formerly enjoyed, tinged now by a sense of mortality. In the joyous rebirth ceremony depicted here in a tomb painting, a priest plays the harp for companions in death.

A detail from *The Book of the Dead*, a sacred text that served as a guide to a holy life, death, and rebirth. Preparing for her fate, Cleopatra requested that her children be permitted to rule Egypt, while she began to investigate the effects of various poisons.

the drugs that acted most quickly caused the victim to die in agony, while the milder poisons took a long time to take effect, she went on to test the lethal qualities of various venomous creatures, which were made to attack one another in front of her. She discovered that the bite of the asp, a snake native to Egypt, brought on a kind of drowsiness and numbness. This would be the best method of suicide if it was necessary. Antony and Cleopatra did make some attempts to ameliorate the harshness of their situation. They both sent messages to Octavian. Cleopatra asked that the kingdom of Egypt be left for her children. Antony requested that he be allowed to live as a private citizen, just as Lepidus had been permitted to retire after his defeat. Antony also offered to retire to Athens if Octavian did not want him to stay in Egypt.

Octavian replied only to Cleopatra. He said if she would do away with Antony or expel him from Egypt, "there was no favor she might not ask." She refused the offer; she and Antony were to remain lovers until death separated them.

As the winter passed, Octavian continued his military maneuvers. He sent troops toward Alexandria from Africa and Syria. Octavian also sent a messenger to assure Cleopatra that he bore her no ill will and to promise that she would not be harmed.

Octavian may have had an ulterior motive for this promise. It was well known that Cleopatra had a vast treasure, not only of gold and silver but also of emeralds, pearls, ivory, ebony, and extremely valuable spices such as cinnamon. Cleopatra had stored this treasure in tombs and monuments near the temple of Isis. Since it would have been easy for her to destroy it or move it far up the Nile to a hiding place out of Octavian's reach, it was in Octavian's best interests not to alarm the Egyptian queen into making such a move.

Octavian, marching with the forces from the east, took the Egyptian outpost of Pelusium. It would not be long before he arrived in Alexandria.

For the moment Antony roused himself from his inactivity and went out to meet the advance guard of Octavian's forces. Antony's men scored a victory — his last — by driving Octavian's cavalry back to their main lines.

Antony rode triumphantly back to Alexandria, rushing into the palace and embracing Cleopatra while still in full armor. During an ensuing victory celebration, Antony pointed out a soldier who had been particularly brave during the battle. As a re-

Cleopatra has been too long viewed through the distorting medium of official Roman propaganda. Whatever her moral failings, she was a woman of outstanding genius and a worthy opponent of Rome.
—ERNLE BRADFORD
modern historian

ward Cleopatra gave the man a gold breastplate and helmet. That same night, however, the honored soldier deserted to Octavian's camp, presumably to be sure of keeping his reward.

Antony next sent Octavian a challenge to fight hand-to-hand to settle their dispute personally. Octavian shrugged this challenge off with the reply that Antony could surely find better ways of ending his life.

The only course now open was for Antony to attack Octavian's force with all the strength he could muster. On the evening before the attack, Antony asked the palace servants to be liberal with the wine, for tomorrow they might have a new master. The Order of Those Inseparable in Death gathered for the last time; they wept in the midst of their feast.

According to legend, the people of Alexandria were awakened that night by the sounds of dancing and singing, as if the city had been invaded by a troop of bacchanals, or revelers. At the city's east gate, the noise became loudest and then stopped. Those who tried to discover a meaning for this omen concluded that the god Dionysus had abandoned Antony.

At dawn, Antony and his forces marched out of the city. He moved to high ground, where he watched in horror as Egypt's small naval force immediately surrendered to Octavian. His cavalry soon did likewise.

Stunned, Antony concluded that Cleopatra must have commanded her fleet to surrender quickly in order to win favor with Octavian. He rode back to the city convinced that Cleopatra had betrayed him to the enemies he had made for her sake.

Fearing his anger, Cleopatra fled to the monument which housed most of her treasure. She sealed herself and two of her most loyal servants inside the well-fortified building. When Antony heard a false report that Cleopatra had killed herself, Plutarch reports that he said to himself, "Antony, why delay longer? Fate has snatched away the only pretext for which you could say you yet desired to live." Antony then asked his servant Eros to carry out his pledge to kill his master if necessary. Unable to strike the blow, Eros instead killed himself.

As Octavian approached Alexandria, Cleopatra hid her vast treasure in tombs and monuments near the temple of her favorite goddess, Isis. These life-size golden goddesses encircled the gold coffin of the pharaoh Tutankhamen, with Isis represented on the left.

"Well done, Eros," said Antony. "You show your master how to do what you had not the heart to do yourself." Then, in Roman fashion, Antony placed the point of his sword against his stomach and fell forward onto the ground. Even in this, however, Antony was not successful — he did not die immediately. When others found him, they quickly carried him to Cleopatra's hiding place. Cleopatra was determined not to be taken alive so she refused to unbolt the door. Plutarch claims that some ropes were lowered from the window for Antony. "The slaves fastened Antony to these and the queen pulled him up with the help of her two waiting women, who were the only companions she had allowed to enter the monument with her. Those who were present say that there was never a more pitiable sight than the spectacle of Antony, covered with blood, struggling in his death agonies and stretching out his hands towards Cleopatra as he swung helplessly in the air."

Once Antony was brought inside, the distraught queen became hysterical, crying and shaking her fists at the heavens. She then threw herself onto Antony. His blood soon covered her garments.

In his play *Antony and Cleopatra*, Shakespeare has Antony say, "I am dying, Egypt, dying. Give me some wine and let me speak a little." Antony advised Cleopatra to trust Proculeius, one of Octavian's men, if he came to Cleopatra with an offer.

According to Plutarch, Antony told Cleopatra she "should not pity him in this last turn of his fate, but rather rejoice for him in remembrance of his past happiness. He had been of all men the most illustrious and powerful, and in the end had fallen not ignobly, a Roman by another Roman overcome." With these words, Antony died.

Just as Antony had anticipated, Proculeius soon appeared outside the sanctuary. Octavian had charged him to keep Cleopatra alive and her treasure intact. Some have speculated that Octavian intended to make Cleopatra the most important trophy in his Roman Triumph.

Cleopatra was wily enough not to open the door. She parleyed with Proculeius, demanding that her

Witnessing the surrender of Egypt's navy to Octavian, in a tragedy of errors, Antony stabbed himself, believing Cleopatra had betrayed him and committed suicide.

children be given the kingdom of Egypt. Proculeius could not promise this, but told her that she could trust Octavian. Cleopatra was prepared to wait for further proof of Octavian's sincerity.

Proculeius devised a plan. While Gallus, a Roman general, distracted Cleopatra's attention by speaking with her through the door at the base of the sanctuary, Proculeius and several of his men used some long ladders to reach an open window high up the monument.

Hearing the screams of her servants, Cleopatra scrambled for a dagger but before she could stab herself, Proculeius's men grabbed her. Now she was Octavian's prisoner.

This engraving appeared on the playbill for a theatrical production at England's Drury Lane Theatre in 1873, and pictures Antony's death scene in William Shakespeare's drama *Antony and Cleopatra*.

Encrusted with lapis lazuli, rubies, and gold, this jeweled emblem was the symbol of the Ptolemies, whose reign came to an end with Cleopatra's death. Fearing that her sons by Caesar and Antony might someday claim the rulership of Rome, Octavian ordered their execution.

Octavian allowed her to bury Antony with honors and all the royal splendor that she could summon. Grief-stricken, she fell into a high fever and refused food, hoping to die. But Octavian, threatening the safety of her children, forced her to take food and medicine.

A few days later Octavian paid Cleopatra a visit. She jumped up from her sickbed, wearing only a thin garment, and flung herself at his feet, "her hair and face looking wild and disfigured, her voice quivering, and her eyes sunk in her head." Plutarch continues, "But, for all this, her old charm, and the boldness of her youthful beauty, had not wholly left her and . . . still sparkled from within."

Cleopatra may have thought that she could yet again overcome a man's will by appealing to his desires. Certainly this is what Plutarch would have us believe. In any case, Octavian resisted her charms.

Plutarch claims that Cleopatra told Octavian her opposition to him had stemmed from her fear of Antony. If she did say this, it was so absurd that Octavian could not possibly have believed it. Cleopatra then was forced to give Octavian an inventory of her treasure. When a less than faithful steward pointed out that she had omitted some items from the list, the infuriated Cleopatra grabbed him by the hair and gave him several blows on the face.

Octavian pulled her off the servant. After regaining her composure, Cleopatra said she could not tolerate being accused of "hiding some women's toys." The items in question were, in any case, not meant for her, but only kept back so that she might have something left to make presents to Octavian's sister Octavia and his wife Livia, so "that by their intercession I might hope to find you in some measure disposed to mercy."

After promising her leniency, Octavian departed. A few days later, however, he sent word that in a short time he planned to return to Rome, taking her

As Octavian's prize captive, Cleopatra was confined to her quarters under heavy guard. She thwarted Octavian's plans to parade her in a Roman Triumph, however, by subjecting herself to the bite of a poisonous snake. Her death is reenacted in this dramatic scene from a 19th-century Shakespearean production, suggesting her ultimate victory — the preservation of her legend.

and her children with him. Memories of her sister Arsinoë, marching in chains at Caesar's Roman Triumph, must have then passed through Cleopatra's mind.

Cleopatra asked for, and received, permission to make offerings at Antony's grave before the trip to Rome. She was carried to the burial place with tears in her eyes. According to Plutarch, Cleopatra lamented, "O, dearest Antony, it is not long since I buried you with these hands. Then they were free, now I am a captive, and pay these last duties to you with a guard upon me, for fear that my just griefs and sorrows should hold back my servile body, and make it less fit to appear in their triumph over you."

After crowning the tomb with garlands and kissing Antony's gravestone, Cleopatra returned to her quarters and ordered a bath and a sumptuous meal. Meanwhile, someone appeared at her door, carrying a basket of figs. Octavian's guards stopped him and made him eat one of the figs to make sure they were not poisoned. They then allowed him to enter. Inside the basket of figs, according to legend, was a deadly asp. After the meal, Cleopatra closed the door to her chamber and wrote a letter to Octavian.

Upon receiving her letter, in which she requested that she be buried beside Antony, Octavian suspected that Cleopatra had attempted suicide. He quickly sent messengers, but they were too late. The queen of Egypt was dead, lying on a bed of gold, dressed in all her royal finery. Her servant Iras was dying at her feet, while another, Charmion, adjusted the crown on Cleopatra's head. One of the messengers asked Charmion, "Was this well done of your lady, Charmion?" She replied, "Extremely well, and as fitting for the descendant of so many kings." Then she too fell dead at her queen's feet.

Some have questioned the story of the asp, and Plutarch admits that no snake was found, "Only," he says, "something like the trail of it was said to have been noticed on the sand by the sea," outside her window. Others have reported that two puncture marks were found on Cleopatra's arm. In any case, when Octavian's Triumph was held, it included pictures of her with an asp at her breast,

> *Give me my robe, put on my crown, I have Immortal longings in me.*
> —from William Shakespeare's play *Antony and Cleopatra*, Cleopatra's final speech

and this is how her death has generally been represented over the last 20 centuries.

Horace, a Roman poet of the time, was hostile to Cleopatra, yet he wrote these lines about her death:

Yet she preferred a finer style of dying:
She did not, like a woman, shirk the dagger
Or seek by speed at sea
To change her Egypt for obscurer shores,

But gazing on her desolated palace
With a calm smile, unflinchingly laid hand on
The angry asps until
Her veins had drunk the deadly poison deep:

And, death-determined, fiercer than ever,
Perished. Was she to grace a haughty triumph,
Dethroned, paraded by
The rude Liburnians? Not Cleopatra.

The Death of Cleopatra, a 17th-century Italian painting by Mazzoni Sebastiani, portrays the dying queen in traditional fashion, holding the asp that released her from captivity.

Further Reading

Balsdon, J.P.V.D. *Julius Caesar: A Political Biography.* New York: Atheneum Publishers, 1967.

Bradford, Ernle. *Cleopatra.* New York: Harcourt Brace Jovanovich, 1972.

Caesar, Julius. *The Civil War.* Baltimore: Penguin Books, 1970.

Franzero, Carlo Maria. *The Life and Times of Cleopatra.* New York: Philosophical Library, 1957.

Grant, Michael. *Cleopatra.* New York: Simon and Schuster, 1972.

Lindsay, Jack. *Cleopatra.* New York: Coward, McCann & Geoghegan, 1970.

Plutarch. *Lives of the Noble Romans,* ed. Edmund Fuller. New York: Dell Publishing Co., Inc., 1959.

Roebuck, Carl. *The World of Ancient Times.* New York: Charles Scribner's Sons, 1966.

Stark, Freya. *Rome on the Euphrates.* New York: Harcourt, Brace & World, 1966.

Weigall, Arthur. *The Life and Times of Cleopatra.* New York: G.P. Putnam's Sons, 1924.

———. *The Life and Times of Mark Antony.* New York: G.P. Putnam's Sons, 1931.

Chronology

Index

Dorothy and Thomas Hoobler have written many histories for young people, including *The Trenches: Fighting on the Western Front in World War I*, which was named a "Best Children's Book of the Year" by *School Library Journal*. They live in New York City with their daughter. They are also the authors of *Joseph Stalin* and *Zhou Enlai* in the Chelsea House series WORLD LEADERS PAST & PRESENT.

Arthur M. Schlesinger, jr., taught history at Harvard for many years and is currently Albert Schweitzer Professor of the Humanities at City University of New York. He is the author of numerous highly praised works in American history and has twice been awarded the Pulitzer Prize. He served in the White House as special assistant to Presidents Kennedy and Johnson.